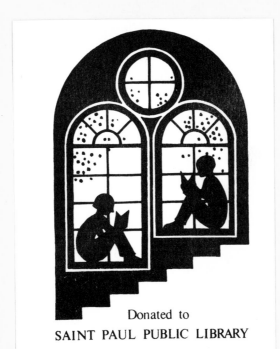

A SENDER OF WORDS

Courtesy Ron Nicodemus

A SENDER of WORDS

Essays
In Memory of John G. Neihardt

Edited by

Vine Deloria, Jr.

HOWE BROTHERS
SALT LAKE CITY   CHICAGO
1984

published by

Howe Brothers — Salt Lake City, Utah

Manufactured in the United States of America

LIBRARY OF CONGRESS CATALOGING IN PUBLICATION DATA

Main entry under title:

A Sender of words.

"A chronology of books by John G. Neihardt": p. x
Includes index.
1. Neihardt, John Gneisenau, 1881–1973—Criticism
and interpretation—Addresses, essays, lectures.
I. Neihardt, John Gneisenau, 1881–1973.   II. Deloria,
Vine.
PS3527.E35Z87   1984   811'.52   84–9054
ISBN 0–935704–22–1

Foreword

CONTINUING A PRACTICE BEGUN when our beloved poet was still with us, old friends and new gathered together in 1981 to share in the reflected glory of another Neihardt Day. Annually, Neihardt Day is held on the first Sunday in August. It is a state holiday, as proclaimed by the governor of Nebraska, and is cosponsored by the John G. Neihardt Foundation and the Nebraska State Historical Society. Around the kitchen table on August 3, 1981 were Ron Hull, master of ceremonies and program chairman for NETV; Vine Deloria, Jr., principal speaker for the day and author of *God Is Red*; Chris Sergel, president of Dramaties Publishing Company and author of the play "Black Elk Speaks"; Bobby Bridger, balladeer-in-residence for the Neihardt Foundation; Angela Rackley; Kay Young; and myself. Over the final cup of coffee, the upcoming centennial celebration of John Neihardt's birthday was discussed. Although plans for the year were complete, our inability to come up with something concrete to honor Neihardt and his work was brought to the attention of these faithful friends.

On the way to the airport, house guest Vine Deloria, Jr., told us he had given our request much thought and asked if a book of commentaries and tributes by some of the best known western writers would comply with our desires. We were delighted. This book is the result of those conversations.

[v]

Foreword

The John G. Neihardt Foundation is a non-profit organization dedicated to the preservation and promotion of Nebraska's Poet Laureate in perpetuity, the late John G. Neihardt.

The Foundation members provide funding for many projects, some of which are books, microfilm, and tapes for the Neihardt Center library; equipment for the audio visual room; and educational brochures for general distribution. The Foundation also accepts gifts of Neihardt and related memorabilia for the Center.

Bancroft, Nebraska is the location of the Neihardt Center and headquarters of the Neihardt Foundation. While the two are separate entities (the Center belongs to the citizens of the state and is managed by the State Historical Society under the direction of Marvin Kivett), our mutual goals make for a rewarding relationship.

We wish to thank the many gracious and talented artists who contributed so generously of their valuable time to this effort. To Vine Deloria, Jr., for conceiving the project, organizing the talent search, and locating a publisher, we are forever in your debt; without your dedication this volume would not exist. To the many people all along the way whose help was needed but whose names remain unsung, please know that we are grateful.

Finally, there is the memory of John G. Neihardt himself. The last fifteen years have been devoted to — aside from tending my family — extolling his virtues. To say that he inspired me to heights I could not have reached otherwise is an understatement. His death left me stunned. It was as though I expected him to live forever. I felt cheated — we had been friends such a short time.

The beautiful Neihardt Center in Bancroft is some consolation. He helped with the planning stages. He approved the design. We shared the joy of a dream come true. Fulfilling our promise to him, we keep the Center alive with programs, workshops, and exhibits. He did not want it to be a place of things only. "Keep it alive with people," he said, and so we shall.

Always when I walk down the good red road and stand at the "tree of life" in the room dedicated to him, I am aware of the promise he made the last time we met. He said, "My eyes will never see the Neihardt Center but my spirit will be there." I believe it. On Neihardt Day, August 5, 1979, six hawks circled slowly over the Sioux prayer garden on the grounds of the Neihardt Center. Was he sending us a message of approval? Or was it Black Elk?

Let others write of his greatness, of his poetry and his many books. I am content to have been his friend.

Marie Vogt
President
John G. Neihardt Foundation, Inc.

Contents

A CHRONOLOGY OF BOOKS BY JOHN G. NEIHARDT

1900   *The Divine Enchantment.* James T. White.

1907   *The Lonesome Trail.* John Lane.

1908   *A Bundle of Myrrh.* Outing.

1909   *Man-Song.* Mitchell Kennerly.

1910   *The River and I.* Putnam.

1911   *The Dawn-Builder.* Mitchell Kennerly.

1912   *The Stranger at the Gate.* Mitchell Kennerly.

1913   *Death of Agrippina.* Poetry Magazine.

1914   *Life's Lure.* Mitchell Kennerly.

1915   *The Song of Hugh Glass.* Macmillan.

1916   *The Quest.* Macmillan.

1919   *The Song of Three Friends.* Macmillan.

1920   *The Splendid Wayfaring: The Exploits & Adventures of Jedediah Smith & the Ashley-Henry Men, 1822–1831.* Macmillan.

1920   *Two Mothers.* Macmillan.

1925   *The Song of the Indian Wars.* Macmillan.

1925   *Poetic Values — Their Reality and Our Need of Them.* Macmillan.

1926   *Collected Poems*. Macmillan.

1926   *Indian Tales and Others*. Macmillan.

1932   *Black Elk Speaks*. William Morrow.

1935   *The Song of the Messiah*. Macmillan.

1941   *The Song of Jed Smith*. Macmillan.

1949   *A Cycle of the West*. Macmillan.

1951   *When the Tree Flowered*. Macmillan.

1953   *Eagle Voice* (English edition of *When the Tree Flowered*) Melrose.

1965   *Lyric and Dramatic Poems*. University of Nebraska.

1971   *Mountain Men*. University of Nebraska.

1971   *Twilight of the Sioux*. University of Nebraska.

1972   *All Is But a Beginning: Youth Remembered, 1881–1901*. Harcourt Brace Jovanovich.

1978   *Patterns and Coincidences: A Sequel to All Is But a Beginning*. University of Missouri.

1984   *The Sixth Grandfather: Black Elk's Teachings Given to John G. Neihardt*. Edited by Raymond J. Demallie. University of Nebraska.

A Bibliographic Note: Many of the above works have had subsequent and multiple editions. In the following articles, the authors have been free to cite the edition of Neihardt's publications which they used. No attempt has been made to correlate page references to *Black Elk Speaks*, for example, with any single edition. Readers should consult chapter notes for the publication date of any edition which is cited.

Introduction

Vine Deloria, Jr.

FOR MANY OF US, JOHN G. NEIHARDT has become the premier western poet. No one has attempted to recapitulate the western historical experience in quite such comprehensive and ambitious terms as he. Nor have many American poets approached his power to invoke a historical period, his vision in discerning the hidden strengths and weaknesses of the human personality, and his wisdom in placing human activities within the larger stage of nature. In the sweep of his epic poetry, virtues often transcend their incarnate form and speak to us of eternal qualities which we like to imagine we all possess in our best moments. Somehow we believe we take strength from Neihardt's poetry and discover that we are only drawing from a reservoir hidden deep within ourselves that we did not know existed until he reminded us.

Neihardt's life was ordinary, his understanding of life was extraordinary. Born in 1881 in Sharpsburg, Illinois, at a time when the frontier was still beckoning to adventurers, Neihardt moved with his mother and brothers and sisters, his father having deserted the family, to Wayne, Nebraska, where his uncle had settled on a farm. When Neihardt was eleven, approximately the same age when Black Elk had his first vision, he had a strange dream in which he felt himself flying through space, in another reality, a reality so complete and tangible that he thereafter devoted himself to the pursuit of poetry and more specifically to reciting the story of western settlement. In view

[1]

of Neihardt's later life, even the skeptic must view this dream as a vocational calling of unusual intensity and clarity.

Like many other poets, Neihardt worked at many jobs, from a newspaper editor, to college professor, federal employee in the Bureau of Indian Affairs, and lecturer. His career was poetry, everything else was a means to engage in that profession. Two towns became the center of Neihardt's universe as a mature adult: Bancroft, Nebraska, where he lived while working on the newspaper, and Columbia, Missouri, where he worked as a college professor. His final days were spent in Lincoln, Nebraska, with much travel to his old haunts and to far-away places where his fame and public demand took him. He never forgot his beginnings and, in fact, it can be said that with all the honors that came to him and all the disappointments, he never pretended to be other than what he had always been, a small-town American with an insightful appreciation of the people who had preceded him on the land.

The range of Neihardt's writings is extensive. He wrote in both prose and lyric verse; he wrote short stories. Two major themes ran through Neihardt's work: the exploration of the High Plains and western mountains and a profound universal mysticism that found unique expression in the various religions of mankind. *A Cycle of the West* is Neihardt's longest work, a series of "Songs" which celebrated the important figures in the fur trade and Indian wars, written in epic poetic style, and this work occupied most of his adult life. Neihardt is best known for two books he did on the Sioux Indians, *Black Elk Speaks* and *When the Tree Flowered*. Although he spent several years mingling with the Omaha Indians who had their reservation at nearby Macy, Nebraska (a town east of Bancroft), Neihardt was not really interested in Indians until he visited the Pine Ridge Reservation in South Dakota. There he interviewed some of the old men, people who could remember the pre-reservation days when they had lived another kind of life. His interviews with the Oglala elders, particularly the medicine man, Black Elk, had a powerful effect on him, and Neihardt strove mightily to tell their story.

Out of the many contacts with the Sioux (actually a diversion from finishing *A Cycle of the West*), came two books: *Black Elk Speaks* and *When The Tree Flowered*. These Indian books are now regarded as masterpieces of the literature on Indians, the standard by which other efforts to tell the Indian story are judged. They brought Neihardt international fame — but not until his twilight years. The first reception of the Black Elk literature was polite but not very enthusiastic. And no one acclaimed them as having importance in the field of religion. Later, as Neihardt entered his eighties, a rush of interest in *Black Elk Speaks* elevated him to the first rank of writers on Indians and religious subjects. His Indian books were translated into many languages, and hundreds of people, mostly young people searching for some kind of religious certitude, made a pilgrimage to his home to talk with him.

Neihardt could not escape the fame which *Black Elk Speaks* brought him, even though his heart was deeply committed to his epic poem about the mountain men. Lucile Aly, his biographer, entitled the chapter dealing with his writing of the *Song of Jed Smith* "The Cosmic Man," and if Neihardt is to be judged as a religious thinker, a good deal of the philosophy of that particular *Song* must be seen as part and parcel of his own religious perspective. There we find a much more cosmic vista, an affirmation of human personality, and vestiges of an overarching cosmic purpose in our affairs. Neihardt did such a good job of translating the Sioux conversations into a prose manuscript that some Indians came to believe that *Black Elk Speaks* was a verbatim transcript of his talks with the old Sioux holy man, and consequently Neihardt has become the interpreter rather than the expositor of Sioux religion, his own views of *A Cycle of the West* being virtually ignored in the process.

Neihardt's writings have universal appeal because he was very careful to place his characters and stories in their proper historical context. The truly human dimension thus emerges from his work and tells its own dramatic storyline. Artificial circumstances are not arbitrarily introduced to enhance the excitement of the reader. Rather, Neihardt precisely describes the situations in which his characters found themselves, allowing truth to indeed become more powerful than fiction. His short stories, admittedly fictional, deal with universal human themes, and each has an ironic twist that calls us to look at the ironies and coincidences of our existence, a task that others accomplish

in more analytical and scholarly tracts which lack the emotional
element that makes us human.

The essays contained within this collection vary considerably.
We asked the various contributors to write a commentary on John
Neihardt and his work, and each writer found a particular aspect which
he or she felt important. The idea was not to seek conformity of praise
for Neihardt or even personal testimonies, although some people felt
that testimony was the most important statement they could make.
The range of topics which came together in this book do collectively
testify to the universal appeal and application of Neihardt's work.
They illuminate us by showing the remarkable spectrum of thoughts
which his writings can produce. Unanimously they reflect the regional
importance of Neihardt in the sense that he has given the western
lands and peoples a unique identity, a task to which he devoted himself
for over ninety years.

Every essay in this book seeks to contribute more to the body of
literature which Neihardt produced. Even the explanations of some
of his themes are less expository and explanatory, and more an additional challenge to writers and thinkers to move toward the vision
which he saw and shared with others. Neihardt was thus more than
a writer and poet, more than a western historian, and more than a
religious mystic. He was himself an intellectual mountain man,
searching through unknown and uncharted landscapes to see what
hidden wonders lay before the human mind. Much of what he says
is familiar to us, but of this familiar landscape we have neglected a
good deal and forgotten much and failed to appreciate even more.
Neihardt's genius may lay in the fact that he made the commonplace
and ordinary struggles of people appear in their true heroic light.
All is But a Beginning was how he characterized his memoirs of his
youth, indicating that the adventure of life always lay ahead of us.
He was, in his own words, "the Splendid Wayfarer."

The Power of John Neihardt

Dee Brown

MY FIRST ENCOUNTER with the epic poetry of John Neihardt came during my sophomore year in college. That is the age when romantic verses most appeal, that time in life when one's senses are the keenest, before cynicism blights our viewpoint of the earth around us, and idealism still flourishes.

I had signed on that spring for a course in the romantic poets, Shelley and Keats and their contemporaries. They were all wonderful singers of the English language. I loved most of it, especially the short poems such as "Ozymandias," "La Belle Dame sans Merci," and "To a Skylark." The short ones were within my frame of reference at that time and place, not too heavily burdened with Greek and Roman mythological references and symbols. I grew up in the southwestern Bible belt and, for understanding, needed metaphors and similes that referred to Old Testament figures instead of Prometheus and his ilk. The nineteenth-century romantic poets seemed to favor obscure mythological creatures, so that the meanings of their images often passed right over my head. Yet I still admired the rhythm and sound of the poems, even though I sensed that something was missing.

One evening in the college library I found the elements that were lacking. To help with living expenses I'd found a job of sorts in the library. Student assistantship they called it, but most of my three hours each day were spent in shelving returned books. On that par-

Dee Brown, author of *Bury My Heart at Wounded Knee* and many other books on western and Indian history, resides in Little Rock, Arkansas.

ticular evening I was trying to slide a volume of poetry onto a shelf when I knocked a brown-clothed book to the floor. On picking it up I read the title: *The Song of the Indian Wars.* John G. Neihardt. The name meant nothing to me, but anything about American Indians always appealed to my imagination and my fascination with the American past. I took the *Indian Wars* back to my little cubbyhole, and at the first chance stole a quick glance inside. It was poetry all right, not about Eurydice or voluptuous Venus or Mount Olympus, but about Crazy Horse, Red Cloud, Fort Laramie, and the Little Big Horn.

When I finished my shelving for the evening I took the book home, and instead of analyzing the sonnets of John Keats as I was supposed to be doing, I read the stirring lines of John Neihardt. Red Cloud and the Bozeman Trail, the Oglalas and the Cheyennes, Lodge Trail Ridge and Powder River, Roman Nose and Beecher Island.

> A thousand Brules followed Spotted Tail,
> Cheyennes, Arapahoes came riding down
> By hundreds;
> Till the little Soldier Town
> Was big with Teepees.[1]

Before that day I had never heard of Fort Phil Kearny or Colonel Carrington or Red Cloud. They had been left out of my American history texts. And here they were, all coming to life, in the strong beat of Neihardt's poetry, his vivid images, exciting actions, and spirited characters. I read much of it aloud, right down to the doom of Fetterman's "eighty-one" and the blizzard that "roared round Fort Phil Kearny mourning for the slain." And then the Wagon Box fight and Beecher's Island. I knew of these latter events, but had never "experienced" them as I did while reading Neihardt's versions.

I went to bed very late that night and dreamed of rawhide creaking upon travaux, lodgepoles skidding and slithering in the sand, of painted ponies weaving on the run, of the Black Hills, and Custer "crying in the wide world's ear what every need and greed could understand." And before I was scarcely awake the next morning I was into "The Village of Crazy Horse."

[1]*Twilight of the Sioux* (Lincoln: University of Nebraska Press, 1971), p. 8.

Meanwhile among the
Powder River breaks
Where cottonwoods and
Plums and stunted oaks
Made snug his village of a
Hundred smokes
Young Crazy Horse was waiting for the spring.[2]

That was my introduction to John Neihardt, and I did not know until many years afterward how deeply these scenes and events were stamped into my consciousness. No reading of the best prose accounts could have done this, but Neihardt's rhythmic pictures became a secret part of me.

John Neihardt must have felt as a young man the same need that I did for poems of great deeds and great human beings. The first book he owned, it has been said, was Tennyson's *Idylls of the King*, obtained as a premium for soap wrappers he had patiently saved. Undoubtedly he was as moved as I was, as a young man, by those tales in verse of kings and knights and romantic ladies, though Neihardt's "knights" of the West were spared the Victorian sentimentality that afflicted Tennyson's Arthurian characters. How would Tennyson have handled Mike Fink and the other Mountain Men, those "horn-locked bulls that strive before the herd," with their thud of knuckles on the jaw, and gushing nostrils and bloody grins? Knights in buckskins they were in Neihardt's epic poems of the fur trappers. But pity Neihardt. As a young man he had no Neihardt to read as I did.

At that time I was unaware of the power of indigenous literature upon young readers, ignorant of how little of it we had back in those days. We knew Mark Twain, of course, and would have put *Huckleberry Finn* at the top of any list of preferred books, but most of the other stars of today were still writing and had not yet been canonized by the academics. Most American poets were from the East and wrote about New England snowstorms and woodland Indians. In that time before superhighways and commercial airlines few of my acquaintances had even seen the eastern United States. What we read or were assigned to read were mostly works that dealt with faraway and ancient events, unfamiliar cultures, alien characters who did not

[2]*Ibid.*, p. 112.

behave the way people we knew should behave. John Neihardt wrote in the idiom we knew, using real people out of the annals of the American West, recreating true incidents, and yet we sensed, even as naive as we students were then, that he was creating literary art. I say "we," because as I later discovered, there were hundreds of readers of my age group who were discovering Neihardt at the same time that I was, but outside our classrooms, alas, not in them.

I went on of course to seek out his other works, *The Song of Hugh Glass* and *The Song of Three Friends*, which were later to become parts of his *Cycle of the West*. The greatest one had not then been written, and years afterward when I discovered that he had first met Black Elk in August 1930, I remembered that I, too, had been searching for something, something I was not sure what, in the Black Hills country, that very summer; but I was only one and twenty and knew nothing of visions and holy men.

One day late in that springtime when I was studying those English romantic poets, I mustered up enough courage to show my secret find, *The Song of the Indian Wars,* to my English professor. He turned the pages without much interest, reading a few lines, glancing at Allen True's contemporary black and white illustrations (yes, many books were illustrated in those good old days before mass production and inflation) and handed it back to me. I don't recall what he said, but it must have been deprecating because I went away feeling sorry for both of us. I did not know then that my idol Mark Twain was not read in the classrooms until many years after he wrote his best books, was in fact shunned by proper and respectable teachers until he was an old man waiting for Halley's Comet to come and take him away.

After I left college, I encountered John Neihardt's work only occasionally. A job had taken me to the eastern United States, and I seldom met anyone who read him there. I once told Dick Cavett that the greatest thing he had ever accomplished was to bring John Neihardt east of the Mississippi River, a feat that he performed with a memorable television interview. But that was not until 1970.

During World War II, I remember finding one of Neihardt's books in a training camp library in Tennessee. It was a miserable rainy Sunday and we had come back from wintry maneuvers that left me not only physically exhausted but spiritless, and after scanning the depressing newspaper headlines about the war in Europe and the Pacific, I felt hemmed in, almost hopeless about the future. Then I began reading *The Song of Three Friends*: Ashley's hundred fur trappers going west.

> From Mississippi to the Western Sea
> From Britain's country to the Rio Grande
> Their names are written deep across the land
> In pass and trail and river, like a rune.[3]

The three friends, the upstream men — Will Carpenter, Mike Fink, and Frank Talbeau — "each gotten of a doughty breed," daring, roaring, and fighting their way across the unknown land. It had nothing to do with the war, or modern weapons and millions of marching men in uniforms. It was of a time long gone, but it restored my spirits, far better than any army surgeon's injection or tonic could have done. When I drifted off to sleep that night I felt full of hope, and said a little prayer of thanks to John Neihardt.

Later, in the last months of the war, I had the good fortune to find another soldier who had read every published line of Neihardt's work. Neither of us realized this when we met, that we were Neihardt fans. We both had been librarians in civilian life, and by some miracle in that pre-computerized era, we finally ended up in an assignment that compared somewhat roughly to our civilian occupations. Martin Schmitt, who became my good friend for thirty years and co-author of a series of photographic histories of the West, was that other soldier. On one of our assignments not long after we met, we worked for several days with an aged but sturdy colonel of ordnance who had been recalled from retirement to examine reports of faulty artillery. Up to that time Schmitt had been rather cool and distant in his attitude toward me. But late one night, after we'd worked for twelve hours straight, we were returning to our barracks, talking idly about the graying colonel who never showed any fatigue. "Gray-bearded, gray of eye and crowned with gray," Schmitt recited spontaneously. "Hey," I cried. "I know that line. *Song of Hugh Glass*." From that moment on we were friends, thanks to John Neihardt.

[3]*The Mountain Men* (Lincoln: University of Nebraska Press, 1971), p. 3.

On another assignment Schmitt and I accidentally discovered a treasure trove of old Signal Corps pictures buried deep in the Pentagon. Among them were hundreds of photographs, drawings and reproductions of paintings relating to the Indian wars of the nineteenth century. We found that we could purchase prints of these and made arrangements to obtain a number of them. The war came to an end about this time, and while we waited impatiently for our discharge papers to arrive we spent our spare time searching out more long-forgotten photographs of Indians in other government agencies.

Originally we had no intention of making a book from them, but one Sunday while we were sorting out our prized items and making trades, the idea hit us almost simultaneously that what we had was the nucleus of a photographic history of the Indian wars. In arranging our text and illustrations in a chronological narrative we gave no conscious thought to the epic poetry of John Neihardt, which had sung of the incidents we were trying to depict, yet I know now that we were influenced subconsciously by the power of Neihardt's vision. Both of us had read and re-read *The Song of the Indian Wars* so it was natural for us to break away from the old stereotypes of American Indians that had dominated our history and literature for more than a century. I am certain that is why our *Fighting Indians of the West* proved to be far more popular than we or our publishers ever dreamed of, and why it remained in print for more than a quarter of a century.

During the following twenty years I published several other books about the West, some concerned with the same events that Neihardt dealt with in his poems, like *Fort Phil Kearny* and *Action at Beecher Island*. It was as if I were following a well-marked pathway designed by a pioneer trail blazer, although I was not conscious of the fact that I was doing so at the time I chose to write the books.

The culmination of the Neihardt influence was *Bury My Heart at Wounded Knee*, his voice being mixed in with the voices of many Indians who spoke in poetic prose while I wrote that book. When I came to the last poignant chapter there was no other way to end it except with the words of Black Elk who spoke through John Neihardt:

> I did not know then how much was ended. When I look back now from
> this high hill of my old age, I can still see the butchered women and

children lying heaped and scattered all along the crooked gulch as plain as when I saw them with eyes still young. And I can see that something else died there in the bloody mud, and was buried in the blizzard. A people's dream died there. It was a beautiful dream . . . the nation's hoop is broken and scattered. There is no center any longer, and the sacred tree is dead.[4]

I have heard it said that on the day John Neihardt died, a hawk came out of the West and circled his house three times and then flew away toward the setting sun. He is out there somewhere, I am sure, in some form or other, aware that his musical words are being read and spoken in some part of this wide earth every hour of every day.

---

[4]*Black Elk Speaks* (New York: Pocket Books, 1972), p. 230.

Neihardt and the Vision of Black Elk

Frank Waters

THIS PASSAGE IS FOR ME one of man's most eloquent utterances:

> Then I was standing on the highest mountain of them all, and round
> about me was the whole hoop of the world. And while I stood there,
> I saw more than I can tell and I understood more than I saw; for I was
> seeing in a sacred manner the shapes of all things in the spirit and the
> shapes of all shapes as they must live together as one being. And I saw
> that the sacred hoop of my people was one of many hoops that made one
> circle, wide as daylight and starlight, and in the center grew one mighty
> tree to shelter all the children of one mother and one father. And I saw
> that it was holy.[1]

It describes the climax of a vision seen in childhood by a member
of a race that was being nearly obliterated by massacres, theft of homelands, and other oppressions by a foreign conqueror. And yet these
words recounting his vision as a now impoverished and aging man,
sounded no note of bitterness and despair. It was as if he had foreseen
the misery still to come to his surviving people — the continued theft
and exploitation of the little land remaining to them as a government
reservation, the injustices and prejudices yet to be suffered as a racial
minority. In this depressing milieu he found the indomitable hope
to endure until the time when all tribes and peoples and races must
as one mankind on one small planet acknowledge the one Higher
Power that is inexorably dictating their eventual unity. This universal

Frank Waters, author of numerous fictional and nonfictional works on Southwestern Indians, lives in Tucson, Arizona.

[1]*Black Elk Speaks* (New York: Pocket Books, 1972), p. 36.

concept expressed by the vision in simple imagery echoes the wisdom of the world's sages and saints from the earliest times.

The vision in its entirety was related by the Oglala Sioux holy man Black Elk to John G. Neihardt on the Pine Ridge Reservation in South Dakota over fifty years ago. It may seem strange that he told this vision to a white man, a member of the race that had ruthlessly crushed underfoot the proud Sioux nation during its imperial march across the North American continent. Yet the Powers Above which mysteriously prescribe the successive rise and fall of nations and civilizations, often pick unwitting agents and spokesmen to further the ever-evolving consciousness of mankind toward transcendent completeness.

Neihardt writes that he had not known Black Elk until the day he was escorted by an interpreter to meet him. The old man, nearly blind, was standing in front of his one-room log cabin. Sitting down, he said to the interpreter Flying Hawk, "I can feel in this man beside me a strong desire to know the things of the Other World. He has been sent here to learn what I know, and I will teach him." When Neihardt left, Flying Hawk said to him, "That was kind of funny, the way the old man seemed to know you were coming."

It was that simple or that complex. There are more things behind such seemingly casual but far-reaching encounters than we can guess. My notes here deal chiefly with the preparation of Neihardt for his task and with Black Elk's Great Vision.

The facts about Neihardt's life are too well known to be repeated here. They are given in his autobiography and the biography of him written by Blair Whitney for the Twayne United States Authors Series. He was born in 1881 in a rented two-room farm shack in Sharpsburg, Illinois. Shortly afterward he and his two older sisters were taken by their parents to Kansas City, Missouri. His father obtained work here, but soon deserted his family. His mother then moved with the children to live with her parents in a one-room sod house in Wayne, Nebraska.

Neihardt's fascination with the great Missouri River stands out as the most prominent feature of his childhood. The river was still the turbulent eastern boundary of the endless expanses of prairie and plains into which thousands of settlers were moving. He knew their life; he had lived it. At the age of thirteen he entered Nebraska

Normal College, completing the course in two years. Becoming a
reporter for the Omaha *Daily News*, he then bought the Bancroft
News. Meanwhile he married Mona Martinsen, whose father had
been president of the Missouri, Kansas, and Texas Railroad. That
same year, when he was twenty-seven years old, John Neihardt under-
took his greatest adventure. He made a 2,000 mile canoe trip with
two companions down the Missouri from Fort Benton, Montana, to
Sioux City, Iowa. It resulted in his first writing of consequence,
an account of his trip appearing as a series of articles in *Outing Magazine*, then as a book under the title *The River and I*.

The book was a simple narrative of high adventure, amusing
incidents, and vivid descriptions of the river and its lands. Yet during
the trip Neihardt experienced the mystery of the great river that had
fascinated him since childhood, reliving its historical ascent by the
Lewis and Clark expedition and the days of the old forts, fur trappers
and Indian traders. All this he saw as a great American epic comparable to the *Iliad* and the *Odyssey*. But where, oh where, was the
Homer to sing its song? So took shape the nebulous outline of his
own future epic, *A Cycle of the West*.

There now came from him a prolific outpouring of verse, plays,
novels, and volumes of his collected poetry. None of them were
markedly successful. To help support his family of four children,
he wrote literary criticism for the St. Louis *Post Dispatch* and the
Minneapolis *Journal*, and gave popular readings of his poems. If his
writings did not gain him national recognition as a writer of any
importance, they earned him a good reputation in his own home
region. One envisions him at the age of thirty as a moderately successful, short and light-boned man with a somewhat professorial look,
comfortably living with his family in small towns in the midwest.
A solid citizen but surely not yet one destined for enduring fame.

He now began work on that American epic which he had envisioned a few years before — a task that took him thirty years to
complete. *A Cycle of the West* celebrates the conquest of the Missouri
River Valley from 1822 to 1890. The *Cycle* is a long narrative in
blank verse, filling some 650 pages and containing 16,000 lines,
a poem as long as the *Iliad* and the *Odyssey*. It is divided into five
poems which were published separately between 1915 and 1941.

The characters of the *Songs* are mountain men, fur trappers, Indian traders, keel boat crews, soldiers, and isolated settlers — men ignorant and brutal, kind and noble, all impelled by the invisible force of "Manifest Destiny" to open the wilderness. And they encounter in the Indian tribes a people equally courageous and religiously dedicated to preserving their homelands against invasion. *The Song of the Indian Wars* and *The Song of the Messiah* contain the best writing in the *Cycle*. The first narrates the campaign against the Sioux and their Cheyenne allies by United States cavalry troops from 1866 to 1877. All the major encounters — Red Cloud's War, the Fetterman fight, the battle of Beecher's Island, Custer's Last Stand on the Little Big Horn — are eloquently described, concluding with the tragic murder of Crazy Horse, the gallant and charismatic Sioux warrior.

The Song of the Messiah carries on the cycle of conquest. The Sioux were now a defeated and betrayed nation. The vast buffalo herds which had supported them had been destroyed. The starving people, herded onto reservations, had lost hope. Then in Nevada appeared a Paiute named Wovoka who claimed to represent the real powers of life and preached of a coming resurrection when the whites would be destroyed and the Indians — and their old way of life — would be restored. The desperate Sioux welcomed this new religion, as did people in other tribes, and began holding the prescribed Ghost Dances which were interim ceremonies believed to assist in bringing about this conclusion to history. The white Indian agents, fearing the dances signalled another conflict, called in Army troops. Sitting Bull was betrayed by reservation intrigue and killed by federal Indian police on the Standing Rock Reservation.

News of the famous old medicine man's death spread terror among his people. A band of 350 men, women and children under the leadership of Big Foot left the Cheyenne River Reservation in central South Dakota and sought refuge at the Pine Ridge Reservation several hundred miles south. They were surrounded by four troops of Custer's rejuvenated Seventh Cavalry and escorted to the base camp on Wounded Knee Creek. Early next morning, on December 29, 1890, they were assembled and ordered to give up their arms. Somehow, by accident, a rifle went off. Then it happened. The surrounding 500 cavalrymen charged in and from the slope above the creek four

Hotchkiss guns hurled two-pound shells into the Indian camp, killing
300 of the 350 Sioux. That night there was a severe blizzard. Not
until New Year's Day could the frozen Sioux bodies be dug out of the
snow and buried in a mass grave on the hillside.

This infamous massacre — which popular history books still call
the "Battle of Wounded Knee" — concludes Neihardt's *Song of the
Messiah*. It also ended all Indian defense of their homelands. In these
two verse narratives Neihardt clearly expresses his understanding and
empathy with the Indians, yet the other three *Songs* in the *Cycle*,
featuring notable mountain men, reveal his natural pride in his young
nation's westward expansion. This ambivalence is balanced by his
depiction of human values common to both peoples.

The initial warm reception of the *Cycle* did not last. The various
books went out of print; not until recently have they been reissued in
one volume. There may be many reasons why they are not very
popular today. For one thing, almost every exploration, every battle
and massacre, every character, has now been exhaustively reported in
documentary histories, novels, and thinly disguised movie versions of
the real events. Neihardt's work, with one great exception, has not
yet been accepted as great literature. His poetry is not ranked with
that of Walt Whitman and later modern poets. He was not a visionary
writer with the mystical insights of Melville, nor a transcendental
thinker like Emerson. Hence none of his lyric poetry, verse plays,
novels, and prose history is considered an enduring classic. Nevertheless, we owe him our grateful tribute for breaking ground when the
subject of Indians was too encrusted with ignorance and prejudice for
other writers to plow.

A Cycle of the West is not a complete epic of the westward movement across all of continental America. The conquest of the upper
Missouri River Valley is but one cycle among many in the larger epic
of the entire West. The conquest of the mighty Colorado matches
that of the Missouri. The tribes of every region fought for their homelands with the same tenacity as did the Sioux. And their defeats were
marked by equal tragedy — the Cherokee Trail of Tears, the Navajo
Long Walk, the great march of Chief Joseph and his Nez Perces when
they were expelled from their sacred Wallowa Valley, the massacres

of the Arapahos and Cheyennes at Sand Creek and the Washita, and of the Apaches at Camp Grant and Massacre Canyon . . .

Who can ever hope to achieve an epic of such scope? But if it is ever written, the cycle of conquest must be followed to its rounded end. It must include not only the tragic decimation of all the Indian tribes, but the disastrous effect upon us, their white conquerors. In despoiling and exploiting the western lands we have become the richest and most materialistic nation in the world. But our alienation from nature has affected us psychologically. We have become spiritually bankrupt. So, belatedly we are now beginning to realize the enduring spiritual truth in the Indian reverence for our common Mother Earth. This realization has resulted in the recent emergence of a national interest in Indian life and religion. And accompanying this interest, an unprecedented resurgence of life and hope among all Indians. Tribes everywhere are demanding and receiving compensation for lands illegally taken from them. And young Indians are searching for spiritual guidance in their own tribal beliefs. The great cycle of the conquest of America is rounding to completion.

This prelude must be considered as our context for reading Neihardt's superlative *Black Elk Speaks*.

Neihardt's many years of writing always have curiously reminded me of Winfield Scott Stratton. For seventeen years he, like thousands of other prospectors, trailed with his pack burro through every range and gulch of the Rockies only to dig barren holes. Then by chance he discovered in a briar patch what he had sought. Gold! So pure it made his Independence Mine the most fabulous in America and Cripple Creek on the slope of Pike's Peak in Colorado the greatest gold camp in the world.

So it was with Neihardt. None of his writings had made a notable strike in the raw material of literature. Then when he met Black Elk he found the treasure he had sought. As mentioned earlier, Neihardt met him in 1930, when he was doing research on *The Song of the Messiah*. The old Oglala Sioux agreed to help him. So Neihardt returned the following year with his eldest daughter Enid, an experienced stenographer, and his second daughter, Hilda. Black Elk's son Ben served as interpreter and several Sioux elders supplemented his dictated narrative with their own versions of events. In developing

Black Elk Speaks, Neihardt summoned all his talent for writing poetry and prose. His great book made him justly famous, was eventually translated into eight languages, and endures to enrich us all.

Unlike the free verse of *A Cycle of the West*, *Black Elk Speaks* is written in prose. It is the autobiography of Black Elk from his early childhood through his participation as a warrior in the Indian wars. The book is more than this chronology. For Black Elk was a visionary constantly in touch with the Other World of the Spirit. His narrative recounts innumerable visions and mystical experiences, but throughout his life Black Elk was possessed by one great vision of incomparably beautiful imagery, complex symbolism, and profound meaning. This Great Vision is of concern to us now. It is the living heart of Neihardt's book as it was of Black Elk's life. Any attempt to describe it would do it injustice; so, in this short outline of its salient features, I have used Black Elk's own words whenever possible, without inserting constant quotation marks.

When Black Elk was four years old he first heard voices from above. A year later he saw the figures of two men coming down from the clouds head first like arrows and singing a sacred song. Thereafter he kept hearing voices calling him. And then, when he was nine years old, came the Great Vision. Outside his tepee he saw the same two men coming from the clouds. Reaching the ground they said to him. "Hurry! Come! Your Grandfathers are calling you!"

A little cloud then picked him up and carried him up to a cloud tepee with a rainbow door. Sitting inside it were six old men, the Grandfathers, the Powers of the World. The Power of the West gave him a cup of water, the Grandfather of the North an herb of power, he of the East a peace pipe, and he of the South a red stick that sprouted branches and blossoms. "Behold the earth!" he said. Black Elk looked down. In the center of the earth bloomed the holy stick that was a tree, marking the crossing of two roads. "A good road on which your nation shall walk," explained the Grandfather. The black road ran west to east. "A fearful road of troubles and of war on which also you will walk. In four ascents you shall walk the earth with power," he concluded.

Now the sixth Grandfather, the Spirit of the Earth, began to speak. He was old, but more as men were old. He slowly changed backwards into a boy and Black Elk recognized him as his own self. When he became old again, he said, "My boy, have courage, for my power shall be yours and you shall need it, for your nation will have great troubles. Come."

And now outside began a great drama of rearing horses. Twelve black horses of the West, four abreast, followed by twelve white horses of the North, twelve sorrels of the East, and the buckskins of the South, all conducting Black Elk on a bay horse along the fearful black road to the east. They came to a village in which the people lay dead or dying. A Voice said: "Behold, they have given you the center of the nation's hoop to make it live." Black Elk, as directed by the Voice, thrust the red stick into the earth. Whereupon it changed into a tall tree beneath whose leafy branches all the birds, animals, and people rose with happy cries.

Black Elk then joined a ghostly procession of his people—a ghostly march of the past and present of the Sioux people. He then made his four ascents and on the fourth ascent found a terrible storm coming. He survived the storm and after the turmoil learned that "All over the universe they have finished a day of happiness."

Once more the riders of the West, North, East and South formed behind Black Elk on his bay horse and they rode east. Ahead loomed high forested mountains flashing all colors upward to the heavens. Then he was standing on the highest mountain of them all, and round about beneath him was the whole hoop of the world. What he saw is described in that wonderful passage quoted at the beginning of these notes.

It is the triumphant climax of his dramatic and apocryphal vision. There is little to add here. He was taken back to the tepee of the Six Grandfathers. Each gave him the gift he had given before— the cup of water and the bow and arrows; the power to make live and to destroy; the white wing of cleansing and the healing herb; the sacred pipe; the flowering stick. The oldest of them said, "Grandson, all over the universe you have seen. Now you shall go back with power to the place whence you came, and it shall happen yonder that hundreds shall be sacred, hundreds shall be flames!"

For years afterward, Black Elk could think of nothing but his twelve-day vision. He told no one what he had seen. A terrible fear began to possess him, for voices kept calling to him, "It is time! It is time!" It seemed that his Grandfathers wanted him to do something. But what? In desperation he told part of his vision to an old medicine man. Black Road reminded him that a man who has had a vision is not able to use his power until he has performed the vision on earth for all people to see. Hence the Horse Dance was performed, with old men representing the Six Grandfathers, four beautiful virgins carrying the four sacred relics, four horses for each of the directions, and a tepee containing a black and a red road. How beautiful it was, though like a shadow of the bright vision itself. Everyone in the village danced and was happy, and Black Elk's fear left him.

What does the vision say to us today?

Two things about it are immediately obvious. Its universality of meaning, and the striking images and symbols which express it. How earthly Lakotan they are! Horses, tepees, trees and grass and clouds, a cup of water, an herb, a red stick. Even the most holy powers above are simply called grandfathers. Yet they all are brought to vivid life in an exciting drama. The story it tells has all the arcane meanings of the world's ancient myths. The Great Vision in whole is a Mystery Play as profound as those of ancient Greece and Egypt. It springs from the earth of America itself, but its roots go down into the unconscious depths of all mankind.

The Sioux believed all the powers worked in a circle. The four quarters were designated by directional colors: red for the east which gave peace and light, yellow for the south which gave warmth, black for the west which gave rain, and the white north with its cold and wind which gave strength and endurance. Crossing this great circle from west to east ran a troublesome black road, and a good red road from south to north. People in their lives symbolically traveled these roads to the four directions, gathering the powers for their full development. These four powers were represented by the four troops of horses which came in Black Elk's vision: the black from the west, the white from the north, the sorrels from the east, and the buckskins from the south.

The pattern thus formed was a cross inscribed within a circle, one of the oldest symbols known to man. Its celestial prototype was formed by the polar constellations in their circuits around the pole star. Wheeling around this one fixed point in the heavens, the constellations described the four arms of the cross dividing the circle into four quarters or quadrants.

Observance of the symbol of the encircled cross and designation of the quadrants by directional colors was not confined to the Sioux. The ancient Mayas and Aztecs, contemporary Hopis and Navajos, as well as Tibetan Buddhists also include directional colors among their religious observances. The Navajo sandpainting of the Whirling Logs forms the pattern of the encircled cross. The cross is formed by two logs, the circle by a rainbow, and the whole is painted in directional colors. The encircled cross is the sign for the Holy Winds Basket in which are laid prayer sticks and cigarettes painted with the colors of the directions. The cross they form within the circular basket is also the sun symbol of Zia Pueblo which, incidentally, has appeared on New Mexican auto license plates.

At the center of the world, where the two roads cross in Black Elk's vision, appears at various times the sacred herb with its four blossoms — blue, white, red, and yellow; the red stick; and the Flowering Tree. The Flowering Tree is the Tree of Life of many world mythologies branching into all mankind's races and peoples. It is the Norse world-tree Yggdrasill, the Tree of Life of the Hebrew Cabbala, and of the Cuna Indians off the coast of Panama, among many others. Perhaps the closest parallel is the tall slim-trunked ceiba with its umbrella-shaped foilage which stood in the center of the ancient Mayas' cosmography. All of these confirm the vision of Black Elk when he saw in the center of the great circle "one mighty tree to shelter all the children of one mother and one father."

Closely allied with the Flowering Tree is the "highest mountain of them all" upon which he stood at the end of his fourth ascent, seeing round about him the whole hoop of the world. It calls to mind the sacred Encircled Mountain which stands at the center of the Navajo's traditional homeland. It is surrounded by four lesser directional mountains, which are readily identified. The location of the Encircled Mountain is known by a small peak, but the Encircled

Mountain itself is invisible. Being the core of the whole cosmos, it existed before the First People emerged from the lower worlds, and spans a time and space beyond our earth-dimensional comprehension. This is its metaphysical reality.

Another striking parallel is found in the cosmography of Tibetan Buddhism. The axis of the cosmos is Mount Meru, shaped like a pyramid with its sides glowing with directional colors. It is said to be eighty thousand miles high and eighty thousand miles deep, containing within it several underworlds and heavens. A lofty peak in the Himalayas bears its name, but it is only a material image, the physical counterpart of the metaphysical Mount Meru.

The functions of the sacred relics in the Great Vision, the healing herb and cup of water, we know. Water nourishes all life, the earth itself. It plays a key role in the mythology and ceremonialism of southwest tribes. Among the Pueblos certain lakes are believed to be places of emergence from the underworld and the abode of spirits, like Taos's Blue Lake, and the Lake of Whispering Waters under which lies the town of Zuni's kachinas. The Tewas along the upper Rio Grande River associate a lake with each of their sacred directional mountains. And huge carved heads of Tlaloc, the Aztec god of water, decorate the ancient Pyramid of Quetzalcoatl in Teotihuacan. The white wing represents the wings of the spirit that carried the sacred pipe on eagle wings and flew Black Elk himself as Spotted Eagle. Archetypal images and symbols, one after another! Little wonder that Carl Jung recommended that *Black Elk Speaks* be translated and published in Germany.

In the last four "ascents" of the vision we encounter an abstract symbolism that may have wide interpretations. Black Elk had traveled to the four horizontal directions. His glimpse behind him of the ghosts of vanished generations of people suggests the element of past time. Now as he begins to climb the four ascents he enters a vertical dimension, and with it the element of future time. Each ascent is more difficult and the plight of his people more pronounced. By the end of the third ascent they are thin and starving, the nation's hoop is broken and a terrible storm is coming. Black Elk, when he had been told of the four ascents he was to make, believed that they meant four generations which he should know, himself being the third. And when in 1931 he related seeing his people's plight and hearing the winds of war fighting like wild beasts at the end of the third ascent, he believed his people had come to that end, and that something bad was going to happen all over the world.

Aside from this premonition of World War II, the four ascents into the cycles of future time have far-reaching parallels. The Mexican Aztecs and Andean Incas, the Zunis, Hopis, and Navajos, Greek mythology, the Zoroastrianism of Persia, the Hebrew Cabbala, and Buddhism, all assert belief in the existence of four successive worlds. The most specific development of this concept was made by the Mayas. With mathematical and astronomical precision they counted timeless time in cycles extending from 52 years to 5,200 years. This Great Cycle measured the duration of each successive world or era. There had been four of these before the present Fifth World according to Mayan belief. The overall duration of all five totaled approximately 26,000 years, the length of the great circle of the precession of the equinoxes — the time required for the vernal equinox to move through the twelve space-and-time divisions of the great circle of the ecliptic.

The Mayas' last Great Cycle was regarded as the duration of the present Fifth World or era. Its beginning the Mayan astronomer-priests projected back to 3113 B.C. and its projected end was 2011 A.D. At this time the world would be destroyed by another catastrophe and superceded by a coming Sixth World. What an astounding prediction to have been made in Indian America 1,300 years ago! And how closely it is paralleled by the present Hopi prophecy which asserts the present world, their Fourth, will soon be destroyed.

The correspondence between these four previous worlds and Black Elk's four ascents opens a wide field of conjecture. In my own opinion the four previous worlds were not physical land masses which were destroyed, but dramatic allegories for the stages of man's ever-evolving consciousness, symbols of cosmic changes taking place in great rhythmic cycles which relate the inner life of man to his vast outer world. If this is true, we too are now facing the last terrible ascent of Black Elk's vision, hearing the winds of war raging like wild beasts around us. Ours is a period of war, revolution, and world-wide change. The twelfth and last 2,160-year Age of the Fish in the zodiacal cycle is ending, and with it also the end of the present great precessional cycle.

What lies ahead? Surely there are signs of the birth of a new way to solve old problems, of a new mode of thought, an expansion of consciousness. Black Elk's spiritual vision offers hope that sometime we too will stand on the highest mountain of all, and see below and around us the hoops of all nations, and growing in the center the great Flowering Tree sheltering all us children of one mother and one father. We can make Black Elk's vision our vision because a humble Nebraska poet came to learn "things of the Other World" and used his considerable talents to bring them to us.

The Poet Beyond Black Elk

Alvin M. Josephy, Jr.

MANY, MANY YEARS AGO, back in the early 1950s, Peter Decker, the eminent New York rare-book dealer, who specialized in the American West and was himself an afficionado of Western American history, urged me to read the works of one John G. Neihardt.

"Why?" I asked.

"Because he is one of our greatest living writers. Oh, Lord," said Peter emphatically. (Peter, as I write this is now 90 and still says, "Oh, Lord," when he wonders why you're so dumb.) "Oh, Lord, it's not just that he's still alive and has written so beautifully about the West, but one hundred years from now his works will be better known than those of most of the writers who are better known than he is today."

I was then embarked on the early stages of a book on the history of the Nez Perce Indians, and was spending a considerable amount of time on research into the activities of the fur trappers and traders who had had contacts with the Nez Perces. I was familiar with Chittenden's studies, with Bernard DeVoto's *Across the Wide Missouri*, and with numerous other published and unpublished sources, and, with help from the late Dale Morgan, who became my good friend and colleague, I was learning particulars about Jed Smith, Hugh Glass, Jim Bridger, "Broken Hand" Fitzpatrick, William

Alvin Josephy, who divides his time between Connecticut, Arizona, and Oregon, is an historian and the former editor of *American Heritage*.

Sublette, David Jackson, and all their contemporaries. But I had never heard of the writings of John G. Neihardt.

Then — thanks to Peter — I waded into *A Cycle of the West.* I was stunned, not alone by the historical knowledge, implying expertise in areas of history that I had thought had only recently been plumbed (Neihardt had begun work on the Cycle in 1912, three years before I was born), but by the heroic majesty and moving human spirit of the *Songs.* Where had this man been — or where had I been — that this was all new to me? Why, in a sound liberal arts education, had there never been a mention of Neihardt — never a line of his writings in any of the anthologies that had been assigned to us, in prep school, at Harvard?

I talked it over with Peter. "Well," he said in his wisdom, "you know the old line, 'a prophet in his own day.'" The material about which Neihardt wrote still appealed only to a small number of readers; the Eastern literary establishment had scant interest in the American West and people who wrote about it, and, as Peter had first said, someday people would discover his writings and recognize his greatness. So I began to recommend to others that they also read *A Cycle of the West.*

Then came the late 1960s and the early 1970s, and the bombshell discovery of *Black Elk Speaks* by a kick-over-the-traces generation of young Americans, both Indian and non-Indian. On campuses and in coffee houses, Indian centers, and bookstores throughout the nation, Neihardt was suddenly revealed and, as quickly, revered. Overnight, it seemed that he was finally receiving the recognition and fame that for so long had been denied him.

But *was* it a firm and enduring unveiling of this great American genius and the power of his works, or was it a transient, and even superficial, love affair with *Black Elk Speaks?* Despite the attention of the media, the embraces of celebrities like Dick Cavett, and the honors from the thousands who applauded his public appearances, something was still being denied him: a sound recognition of his stature as a giant among American literary figures.

Some of those who wrote glowingly about him during the heyday of the fame and influence of *Black Elk Speaks* referred to a "Neihardt cult of young students, poets, mystics, devoted friends who surround him." They talked of "The white man with an Indian heart." All true. But Indians were "in," young people especially wanted to know more about them, and *Black Elk Speaks*, with its moving message of human dignity and brotherhood among all men, was their modern-day *McGuffey's Reader* and Bible, opening their eyes to a new and higher morality.

I must confess to a little skepticism about what was going on. I was overjoyed by the respect and honors finally accorded Neihardt while he was still alive to receive them, and by the way in which *Black Elk Speaks* was introducing to millions of non-Indians the true values and insights and cultural aspects of Native American life. All of that was long overdue, and it was well and good.

But the word "cult" kept sticking in my craw; it implied something temporary and less than whole. Where — especially among those who were still not interested in Indians — was a recognition of Neihardt the poet, Neihardt the man of letters? Where, even among those who newly venerated him, was there an awareness of, and an interest in, the stirring *Cycle of the West*?

Increasingly, I feared that the "discovery" of Neihardt was in reality a discovery of Black Elk, that Neihardt, with all his modesty, humility, and grace, was looked upon at best as the modern-day embodiment and interpreter of the inspiring philosophy and morality of the Indian, and at worst as a performer temporarily titillating superficial and restless counterculture youths. This is not to detract from the grandeur and importance of *Black Elk Speaks*, or to lessen by one whit my own appreciation of, or debt to, Neihardt the poet and Neihardt the human being. But what I wondered — and still wonder — was whether proper recognition had yet come to Neihardt and if not, why not?

In large measure, it appears to me, his public flowering of a decade or so ago was more reflective of the contemporary interest in Indians and the rebellious time in which it occurred than of a genuine nation-wide acceptance of an overlooked poet of the first magnitude. There was something trendy and false even among many of those who flocked around him, clutching *Black Elk Speaks* to their breast. They enfolded Neihardt as a prophet who preached an attractive Indian message, including values and ways of life that many of them did not know, and did not want to know, had long since been corrupted and changed, and existed no more. *Black Elk Speaks* inspired them, and that was good. But when, in one way or another, they became disillusioned or lost interest in the message, as they have done since the 1970's, then did the poet remain, looming large, or did the interpreter and prophet shrink back among a smaller audience?

Perhaps, because of *Black Elk Speaks*, Neihardt the man of letters is better known and more widely appreciated today than he was when Peter Decker first introduced me to his work in the early 1950's. But is he yet in the anthologies, is he yet included among the great American literary figures read and studied in all American literature classes, is he yet recognized, even by name, among most literary critics in the Western cities? Save for an awareness by a precious few that he wrote a book about an Indian named Black Elk, and an abiding admiration and respect by an even smaller number of devotees, I think that he is still largely overlooked and ignored.

If I am right, I would like to know why he does not tower among his fellow Americans. His writings pulsate and beat with the spirit of America. His *Cycle of the West* surely inspired many other writers, including myself (offhand I can immediately think also of Frederick Manfred, as another example), and his *Black Elk Speaks* inspired a good part of an entire generation. Why, if I am correct, is his full work still so unknown?

Friends have ventured that it is because he is a Western writer who wrote on Western themes, and neither have much interest for the so-called Eastern literary establishment. I think that is incorrect. Beginning, perhaps, with Owen Wister's *The Virginian* one can point to Western themes that have been taken seriously by the rest of the country. Western writers have also not fared badly. One can quickly reel off such names as Willa Cather, Wallace Stegner, Carl Sandburg, Mari Sandoz, John Steinbeck, Theodore Dreiser, Gary Snyder, Scott Momaday, Leslie Marmon Silko, and so on.

Others have said that Neihardt the man was too shy, too modest, too self-effacing to seek national recognition for himself. Bah! The implication is that recognition depends on an ability to promote oneself. I prefer to think not, but to trust that the work speaks for itself.

Finally, it has been said that Neihardt's Homeric-style, epic poetry is "too hard to read" for a popular following. What does that mean? Such an explanation has to be nonsense. Is Walt Whitman too hard to read? Or even Homer?

Ultimately — eventually — we who know and read and reread his work have faith that whatever has kept him from acquiring recognition as one of America's greatest poets will disappear, and that his sublime art, as well as his "Indian heart," will speak for itself to all Americans.

To Save a Great Vision

N. Scott Momaday

SEVERAL YEARS AGO, in southwestern Oklahoma, I spent a summer afternoon in the company of a very old and beautiful woman whose name was Ko-sahn. I have written elsewhere of her and of that afternoon. It was an extraordinary experience for me, one that I know now to have been a high point in my life, a moment of singular honor and privilege and humility. It seemed so at the time, of course, but it seems far more so now; my conviction has deepened steadily over the years. Ko-sahn was a Kiowa, a member of my tribe, and she was a close friend of my Kiowa grandmother. Her life was a long one. She was, she reckoned, a hundred years old when I met her. Her life reached across a whole and crucial period in the history of the Great Plains. She was witness to that history, largely unwritten still. But she could speak directly from memory of things that had long since passed into legend and she knew every intimate detail of events long forgotten by the mass of people. There was about her the unmistakable presence of that which is sacred. She was a keeper of the sacred past.

John Gneisenau Neihardt must also have had the sense that he had entered into the realm of the sacred when he visited Black Elk in May 1931 on the Pine Ridge Indian Reservation in South Dakota. Earlier, on the occasion of their first meeting, Black Elk had said to him:

N. Scott Momaday, novelist, artist, and poet, is a member of the Department of English at the University of Arizona.

There is much to teach you. What I know was given to me for men and it is true and it is beautiful. Soon I shall be under the grass and it will be lost. You were sent to save it, and you must come back so that I can teach you.[1]

If this statement surprised the Nebraska poet he did not acknowledge it. Neihardt accepted this trust more than willingly. If the old Sioux holy man's chief purpose in seeing Neihardt was, as he said, "to save his Great Vision for men," Neihardt would be the instrument of preservation devoting his considerable talents to the task. Here is one of the truly fortunate collaborations in our American heritage, bridging times, places, and cultures.

It is through the intercession of John Neihardt, then, that we have access to a principal world view of one of the major tribes of American Indians. *Black Elk Speaks* is now deservedly recognized as a classic in literature by teachers in our high schools and universities. We know this without knowing what the book is, exactly, without knowing precisely where to place it in our traditional categories of learning. Such rubrics as Literature, Anthropology, Folklore, and Religious Studies, not to mention American Studies, and Native American Studies, seem equally appropriate frames of reference, immediate contexts in which the book exerts its prominence. Indeed, the book bears importantly upon all of these categories and more.

But we need not concern ourselves with labels here, any more than we need concern ourselves with the question of authorship or the quality of translation or transcription. It is sufficient that *Black Elk Speaks* is an extraordinarily human document — and beyond that the record of a profoundly spiritual journey, the pilgrimage of a people towards their historical fulfillment and culmination, towards the accomplishment of a worthy destiny. That the pilgrimage was in a tragic sense abruptly ended at Wounded Knee in 1890, that Black Elk's words at last take a tragic turn — "There is no center any longer, and the sacred tree is dead" — is of little consequence in the long run, I believe. For in that sudden and absolute investment in the tragic, in the whole assumption of a tragic sense, there is immeasurable vindication, the achievement of a profound and permanent dignity, an irreducible impression on the records of human history.

[1] *Black Elk Speaks* (Lincoln: University of Nebraska Press, 1970), p. x.

I have stated above that I believe *Black Elk Speaks* is preeminently a human document. By this I mean not that this account tells us of the Oglala Sioux, or even that it reveals to us the extraordinary man Black Elk (or, indeed, that other extraordinary man, John Neihardt), but that it tells us of ourselves and of all humankind. I am interested in the universal elements of the narrative, first as an example of oral tradition, than as literature.

Black Elk's account, of course, is centered in the oral tradition. What does this mean, exactly? It means that the storyteller is illiterate and that his understanding and his use of language are determined by considerations of which we, who function within the written tradition, are only vaguely aware at best. If we are to understand the basic, human elements of Black Elk's account, we must first understand what those considerations are.

Black Elk is first and foremost a storyteller. I use that term advisedly. In the oral tradition the storyteller is he who takes it upon himself to speak formally, as Black Elk does in this case. He assumes responsibility for his words, for what is created at the level of his human voice. He runs the risk of language, and language is full of risks — that it might be miscarried, that it might be abused in one or more of a thousand ways. His function is essentially creative, inasmuch as language is essentially creative. He creates himself, and his listeners, through the power of his perception, his imagination, his expression, his devotion to important detail. He realizes the power and beauty of language; he believes in the efficacy of words and is careful to use them with precision remembering their efficacy. He is a holy man; his function is sacred. He is the living bridge between the human and the divine.

Perhaps we can better examine these matters if we look at a specific passage. Early on in Black Elk's story he recounts the following incident:

> It was when I was five years old that my Grandfather made me a bow and some arrows. The grass was young and I was on horseback. A thunder storm was coming from where the sun goes down, and just as I was riding into the woods along a creek, there was a kingbird sitting on a limb. This was not a dream, it happened. And I was going to shoot at the kingbird with the bow my grandfather made, when the bird spoke

and said: "The clouds all over are one-sided." Perhaps it meant that all the clouds were looking at me. And then it said: "Listen! A voice is calling you!" Then I looked up at the clouds, and two men were coming there, headfirst like arrows slanting down; and as they came, they sang a sacred song and the thunder was like drumming. I will sing it for you. The song and the drumming were like this:

> "Behold, a sacred voice is calling
> you; All over the sky a sacred voice
> is calling."

I sat there gazing at them, and they were coming from the place where the giant lives (north). But when they were very close to me, they wheeled about toward where the sun goes down, and suddenly they were geese. Then they were gone, and the rain came with a big wind and a roaring.

I did not tell this vision to any one. I liked to think about it, but I was afraid to tell it.[2]

It seems to me that such a passage as this one reflects very closely the nature and character of oral tradition, especially the American Indian oral tradition. Taken as a whole, this account appears to be more or less like other vision stories in the same tradition. Let us consider, for the sake of comparison, this somewhat similar Kiowa story.

Long ago there were bad times. The Kiowas were hungry and there was no food. There was a man who heard his children cry from hunger, and he went out to look for food. He walked four days and became very weak. On the fourth day he came to a great canyon. Suddenly there was thunder and lightning. A voice spoke to him and said: "Why are you following me. What do you want?" The man was afraid. The thing standing before him was covered with feathers. The man answered that the Kiowas were hungry. "Take me with you," the voice said, "and I will give you whatever you want." From that day Tai-me has belonged to the Kiowas.

Both narratives proceed from a cosmology inherent in the Plains culture, a cosmology at the center of which is the Sun Dance. Both narratives proceed then from a vested interest in the so-called Vision Quest — proceed from, perpetuate, and celebrate that ideal. In both narratives the vision (and with it the invisible voice; we must not lose the force of the oral, audible element) is paramount. In both,

[2]*Ibid.*, pp. 18–19.

that which is seen is strange and unaccountable. And both stories are extremely portentous. Both of these accounts are revelations, but what is revealed is suspended in doubt. The meaning of these stories is not to be discovered at once. The quest extends not only to the vision but most importantly beyond it to the central meaning itself. Finally, both questers after visions are afraid, the one of what he sees, the other to tell of what he has seen. This detail of being afraid underscores the supernatural center of the vision and of its relation in language as well. The vision *and* the story in which it is conveyed are intrinsically powerful.

The Kiowa story is self-contained. Black Elk's account is, of course, the fragment of a much larger whole. Notwithstanding, there is a perceptible integrity even in the fragment and little if any extraneous matter. The implications and consequent meanings of the passage are important. That the gift of a bow and arrows should come from a grandfather, that the arrows should prefigure the two men in the vision, that the sacred voice "all over the sky" which informs the sacred song should anticipate a rain storm complete with "a big wind and a roaring" — these things are entirely in keeping with both the structure and character of oral tradition.

The attitude of the storyteller towards his story is in the oral tradition appropriately formal. Black Elk stands apart from his story in a sense. He is careful not to intrude upon it. It is not a personal story, not autobiographical essentially; essentially it is a testament. The telling of the story is a spiritual act, and the story-teller has a profound conviction of the religious dimension in which the act is accomplished. Everything comes together in the telling of the story, forming a fabric of whole cloth yet distinguishing elements in their particularity. A passage from *Black Elks Speaks* vividly illustrates the complex interweaving of elements which form this seamless religious garment:

> You have noticed that everything an Indian does is in a circle, and that is because the Power of the World always works in circles, and everything tries to be round. In the old days when we were a strong and happy people, all our power came to us from the sacred hoop of the nation, and so long as the hoop was unbroken, the people flourished.
>
> The flowering tree was the living center of the hoop, and the circle of the four quarters nourished it. The east gave peace and light, the south

gave warmth, the west gave rain, and the north with its cold and mighty wind gave strength and endurance. This knowledge came to us from the outer world with our religion.

Everything the Power of the World does is done in a circle. The sky is round, and I have heard that the earth is round like a ball, and so are all the stars. The wind, in its great power, whirls. Birds made their nests in circles, for theirs is the same religion as ours. The sun comes forth and goes down again in a circle. The moon does the same, and both are round. Even the seasons form a great circle in their changing, and always come back again to where they were.

The life of a man is a circle from childhood to childhood, and so it is in everything where power moves. Our tepees were round like the nests of birds, and these were always set in a circle, the nation's hoop. a nest of many nests, where the Great Spirit meant for us to hatch our children.[3]

I point to this passage in particular, not only because it is an eloquent explication of the Lakota world view at its center with the synthesis of everything gathered together in its unity, but also because it describes the shape of the story itself. Implicit in this passage is the acknowledgement that language, too, is circular. Words follow one upon another, and in the formulation of meaning they return upon themselves. *Black Elk Speaks* is a remarkable example of this principle. It is the circumference of itself; it begins and ends at the same point. It is to Neihardt's credit that he intuitively perceived the underlying structure of the oral tradition and instead of delving into it to discern historical or philosophical truth, merely helped to assist the story to achieve its final polished form.

So the story begins with a reflective mood in which the old man establishes the basic shape of the narration:

. . . These things I shall remember by the way, and often they may seem to be the very tale itself, as when I was living them in happiness and sorrow. But now that I can see it all as from a lonely hilltop, I know it was the story of a mighty vision given to a man too weak to use it; of a holy tree that should have flourished in a people's heart with flowers and singing birds, and now is withered; and of a people's dream that died in bloody snow.[4]

And so the story is begun. And in the end it comes round to this:

[3]*Ibid.*, pp. 198–200.
[4]*Ibid.*, pp. 1–2.

I did not know then how much was ended. When I look back now from this high hill of my old age, I can still see the butchered women and children lying heaped and scattered all along the crooked gulch as plain as when I saw them with eyes still young. And I can see that something else died there in the bloody mud, and was buried in the blizzard. A people's dream died there. It was a beautiful dream.[5]

Thus there is a consistent symmetry in Black Elk's account. He is at every moment aware of the aesthetic foundation of the storyteller's function. He orders his words. He fashions his language according to ancient conceptions of proportions, design, and perspective. The aesthetic realization of his story is not immediately of his own invention. Rather he fits his narrative into the universal scheme which ensures that it will complete itself of its own accord. The motion of his voice is the motion of the earth itself. Everything returns to its origin and in becoming circular establishes its own unity and integrity.

To the extent that Black Elk re-creates his vision in words, he re-creates himself and in so doing re-affirms himself. He also affirms that he has existence in the element of language, and this affirmation is preeminently creative. He declares, in effect: *Behold, I give you my vision in these terms, and in the process I give you myself.* In the ultimate achievement of the storyteller's purpose, he projects his spirit into language and therefore beyond the limits of his time and place. It is an act of sheer transcendence. Spiritually he will survive as long as his words survive. He inhabits his vision, and in the telling his vision becomes timeless. The storyteller and the story told are one.

John Neihardt was a man of letters; indeed he was a poet and he was an epic poet. His poet's sensibility must have made him peculiarly receptive to Black Elk's recitation and the measured cadence of Black Elk's words must certainly have informed him that here was a substance unique in its own kind. Even though he could not understand the language that Black Elk spoke, we cannot doubt, I think, that he discerned quite readily the rhythms, the inflections and alliterations of the holy man's speech. And this discernment was worth a great deal. Without it the book would have lapsed into mere biography of an Indian. With the rhythms and pacing well reproduced, we have a masterpiece of transformation of the oral tradition from

[5]*Ibid.*, p. 276.

one language and culture into another without the loss of the essential spirit of the original narration. Consider the rhythm of this paragraph:

> Late in the Moon of the Dark Red Calf or early in the Moon of the Snowblind, Spotted Tail, the Brule, with some others, came to us. His sister was Crazy Horse's mother. He was a great chief and a great warrior before he went over to the Wasichus. I saw him and I did not like him. He was fat with Wasichu food and we were lean with famine.[6]

The quality of writing here is essentially poetic. Consider the sustained hissing of the "s" sounds throughout, or the alliteration in the final sentence. But I mean not only the immediate quality which informs the translation, but also that fundamental quality which inheres in the substance and integrity of the statement itself. The lyrical names, the precise ordering of detail, the evocation of the great warrior ideal, these constitute a kind of common denominator whose fundamental nature is affirmed by the mere arrangement of them in the speech. These things constitute a kind of common denominator which establishes a bridge between the poem and the sing, between literature and legend, between the written tradition and the oral tradition. The transformation of speech into writing (and particularly *this* speech into *this* writing) is a matter of great importance, I believe. And Neihardt believed it also. He brought extraordinary care, sympathy and dedication to his task of faithfully reproducing the essence of the speech.

There are elements of risk and responsibility here; such is the nature of language. And in the oral tradition these factors are crucial and pervasive. It is the principle of oral tradition that words and the things that are made of words are tentative. A song, or a prayer, or a story, is always but one generation removed from extinction. And the listener must always be keenly and constantly aware that what he or she has heard has been properly and responsibly understood for it is in the transmission over many generations of the essence of human experience that makes the oral tradition so powerful. After Black Elk had recited for John Neihardt the tradition of how the sacred pipe was received by the Lakota, he paused briefly to gauge the impact of his words on the poet. Then he cautiously proceeded:

[6]*Ibid.*, p. 116.

This they tell, and whether it happened so or not I do not know; but if
you think about it, you can see that it is true.[7]

In this cosmic instant, if there has been a meeting of mind and spirit,
the oral tradition bridges the gulf between cultures and establishes
itself in its rightful place.

The risk of loss is constant, therefore, and language is never to be
taken for granted. By the same token the story teller, the man who
takes it upon himself to speak, assumes the responsibility of speaking
well, of making his words count, of gathering together the real meanings and presenting them correctly and appropriately. The spoken
word is the means by which he must keep alive his way of life and
this is a serious undertaking. There is no other possibility of cultural survival.

I am making the case that a certain spirit of language informs the
oral tradition and gives it a power incomprehensible to many people
raised in the literate tradition. It is very likely beyond us, who are
committtted to a written tradition, to say what that spirit of language
is, exactly. But in some sense we can bring ourselves to recognize that
it exists, and under certain circumstances we can even be true to it,
more or less. It certainly isn't an easy task or a facile admission; it
requires a remarkable effort and a profound act of the imagination to
participate in the oral tradition. But it is well worth the effort and
the imagination.

John Neihardt was committed to a written tradition, and his com-
mitment was greater than most people similarly engaged. He made
much good of it in his lifetime. In *Black Elk Speaks*, he exceeds his
tradition for a moment and makes that moment live forever thereafter.
He is made the gift of another man's voice, and he allows us to hear
it distinctly, in the full realization of its meaning.

My day, I have made it holy.

Like the sun of this song, which sanctifies the day in its light, Black
Elk makes holy his story in the telling. The sacred vision is preserved
"for men." For this task, successfully completed, among other things,
we owe to the poet John Neihardt our best thanks.

[7]*Ibid.*, p. 4.

Those Western American Darks

Frederick Manfred

I FIRST HEARD ABOUT JOHN G. NEIHARDT in the summer of 1943.
I was paging through *A South Dakota Guide*, compiled by the Federal Writers' Project of the Works Progress Administration and
published by the South Dakota Guide Commission (Pierre, 1938),
when my eye was caught by a drawing on page 210 showing a mountain man being clawed by a bear. A huge she-grizzly loomed over
him, ready to strike again. Up the gully a few yards were two cub
bears. The cubs were sniffing the air and wondering what all the
roaring was about.

I read the story that accompanied the drawing. It told of Hugh
Glass, mountain man, who'd been horribly clawed and mauled by
the she-grizzly and left for dead by two companions. After he regained
consciousness, he discovered he had a broken leg. Yet somehow,
miraculously, he managed to crawl some hundred miles from the
Grand River to the safety of Ft. Kiowa on the Missouri. Once he
had recovered his health, he set out on a mission of revenge to get the
two men who'd deserted him. What particularly caught my eye was
that at the end, after all was said and done, Hugh Glass let the men go.

The account then quoted John G. Neihardt: "And that fact raises
his story to the level of sublimity." I couldn't have agreed more. I'd
been reading the Greeks — Homer, Aeschylus, Sophocles, Euripides
— and it struck me that Hugh's story was every bit as heroic as that

Frederick Manfred is a novelist, author of *Lord Grizzly* among others, and
resides in rural Minnesota.

of Achilles or Ulysses, and he was even more noble for forgiving the
two men who deserted him.

The next paragraph in the *Guide* read: "John G. Neihardt, poet
laureate of Nebraska, immortalized this feat in *The Song of Hugh
Glass*. On the hill 0.5 miles south of the forks of the Grand, is the
monument with the following inscription:

1823 – 1923

This altar to courage was erected by the Neihardt club August
1, 1923, in memory of HUGH GLASS who, wounded and deserted
here, began his crawl to Ft. Kiowa in the fall of 1823.

At the time I had a good start on my second novel, *Boy Almighty*
(1945), and was busy getting ready to write *This Is the Year* (1947),
my third; but I thought the story important enough to make a note
of it and put it in a separate file. Later I went to the University of
Minnesota Library, near my home, to have a look at Neihardt's *Song*.

The University Library in those days allowed one to inspect a book
before taking it out. A library page got *The Song of Hugh Glass* for
me, and I sat down on one of the hard oak benches near the registration desk and began looking through it. Right away I had an uneasy
feeling about the form in which Neihardt had cast the story. My head
was still full of Homer, and this was not a good imitation of him.
In hoary old days long stories were told in epic poems, but after
Cervantes we had the epic prose novel and could use that form to tell
a story. Sitting on that hard oak bench, I regretted that Neihardt had
chosen an antiquated form. The epic poem really did not fit our nation
or our wild frontier.

I also realized that I probably shouldn't read Neihardt's version.
Because sure as the devil, reading it, I'd be pulled in the direction of
the story line he'd chosen. I'm very impressionable and have always
had to be very careful about that. I remembered how my dad used to
cuss when someone else had been the first to drive down a dirt road
after a rain, leaving a wriggling set of ruts. My father either had to
follow the ruts of the other fellow or somehow straddle them if he
wanted to make his own. And even if he were to make his own set
of ruts, he'd still have to allow for where the other fellow had gone
first. So I read only a few more pages in the *Song*, rapidly thumbed

through the rest, then snapped the book shut and brought it back to the registration desk. I'd make my own set of ruts down that road.

Before I left the library that day, though, I went over to the reference librarian and asked her to keep an eye out for any material on Hugh Glass and General Ashley. Later I bought a copy of the *Guide*. I kept running into Neihardt's name while I studied the mountain man times, reading Chittenden, Doane Robinson, Denig, Larpenter, Parkman, books published by the Smithsonian, the Bureau of American Ethnology, Hodges' *Handbook of American Indians*. Neihardt was an important figure in Western American literature, and I made up my mind that someday I'd have a look at his work. In 1953, after ten years of gathering notes, of thinking and brooding about Hugh Glass, and of learning as much as I could about Indians and mountain men, I finally began the book which became *Lord Grizzly* (1954).

But it was later that I read Neihardt. When I decided to go after an idea involving the Yankton Sioux, in which there would be no white men, I decided I'd better have a look at Neihardt's *Black Elk Speaks*. I had already found Joseph Epes Brown's *The Sacred Pipe*, which is also based on Black Elk's teaching. I examined *Black Elk Speaks* in the reference room of the library, mostly to check it against Brown's version. But in some respects I'm an ornery cuss. A streak of stubbornness kept me from looking more closely into Neihardt's book. Brown was an anthropologist, but Neihardt was a creative artist, and I want to do things alone, be on my own as much as possible, not lean on the efforts of artists in my own field.

Just before I began writing *Conquering Horse* (1959), I ran into some good Indian resources, two of them very important: Andrew High Pine of Pine Ridge and Angela Fiske of Standing Rock. Listening to them, I was persuaded I didn't need *Black Elk Speaks*. Angela Fiske in particular was wonderful — in her seventies, and her memory was still sharp and vivid. She had been raised by a woman who was a little girl when Lewis and Clark passed through, a woman basically uncontaminated by white contact of any kind, and Angela's head was filled by true Indian myth and lore.

In the fall of 1963, I learned that Neihardt was at the University of South Dakota, to make some television tapes at KUSD, the university station. I knew Martin Busch, the director of public broadcasting at USD. I called him up to ask if it would be all right if I drove down from Luverne to meet Neihardt, and would he introduce me to him. Busch thought it a great idea and said to come on down.

I still hadn't read *The Song of Hugh Glass*, and so on the way, I stopped at the Sioux Falls Book and Stationery and bought a copy of *A Cycle of the West*. Armed with that I continued down to Vermillion. But when I arrived at the studio, I was met by an embarrassed Martin Busch. He kept giving me excuses why it wasn't convenient at the moment to meet Neihardt. He took me out for coffee. He took me with him to run an errand for his wife. When we got back, and I finally pushed my way into the control booth at the studio, Busch became very discomfited.

Looking down through the big wide glass into the studio below, I got my first glimpse of Neihardt. "Lord," I thought, "a short fellow; yet sitting down he looks tall." He reminded me of tough runty cowboys I'd met. But he also had the leonine head, flowing gray hair, a noble way of holding himself erect. I was impressed.

Again I said to Busch, "You know, there's something going on here. Why can't I see him?"

Busch finally came out with it. "Well, we were afraid of what might happen when you two met. When we told him you wanted to meet him, he said he wasn't interested. When we asked him why not, he said he'd been thinking of suing you."

"For godsakes! Why?"

"He thinks you stole your idea for *Lord Grizzly* from his *Song of Hugh Glass*."

"But the story of Hugh Glass is in history. You can find it in that old newspaper *The Missouri Intelligencer*. You can find it in Hiram Chittenden's two-volume work on the Old Far West. It's everywhere. Anybody has the right to write about Hugh. Neihardt doesn't own him."

"Well, he's still thinking of suing you."

"That's ridiculous," I exclaimed. "The Greeks never worried about such things. They borrowed left and right from Homer, they borrowed from each other, they wrote about the same themes *ad infinitum*, and there's no record that they ever thought of suing each other."

"Then you never read *The Song of Hugh Glass*?"

"No. In fact, I just now, today, on my way down here, bought the book for him to autograph. Look."

Busch was still uneasy. "Well, I don't think you should meet him."

I sat with my thoughts for a while.

Finally I made up my mind. There's nothing like a confrontation, brain to brain. The moment they were through with the next take, I pushed my way downstairs and approached Neihardt. He was sitting in a swing chair. He saw me coming, and for a moment he stiffened slightly. I held out my hand and said, "John Neihardt? I'm Frederick Manfred, and I hear you're mad at me."

His head moved back an inch. "Oh," he said. "Well, maybe I'm not mad at you."

"I've long wanted to meet you," I said. I held my hand out.

A little smile, a Plains smile, broke out on his weathered wise old face. "Okay." And we shook hands.

"Look," I said after a moment, "I brought this along for you to autograph. I just today bought it in Sioux Falls. Your *Cycle of the West*. Could you?"

Without hesitation he took the book, got out a pen, and inscribed it, "With good wishes for Fred Manfred — John G. Neihardt, Nov. 23, 1963."

Later on, we talked about our problem. He said he'd been disturbed by the many similarities between his *Song* and my *Lord Grizzly*. When I suggested that might have come about because we pretty much used the same sources, he agreed. We had both consulted the South Dakota State Historical Society; we'd both seen the only copy of Hugh's handwriting there; we both knew Will Robinson, son of Doane Robinson and present curator at the Society. I assured him that I hadn't read his version of Hugh's story, except for the opening lines, and that I had my reasons for doing so. I related the story of my father's cussing when someone laid a track ahead of him. He told me friends of his had urged him to sue, that his lawyer daughter Mrs. Hilda Petri had been quite upset when she read *Lord Grizzly*.

Busch and the others watched us, holding their breath. But when he signed my book, they all relaxed. It was the way my father and mother handled their problems with relatives and neighbors — and they always tried to do it on the same day they found out about a problem, before the sun set on it. I hadn't done anything wrong and the only way to settle our differences was to sit down and talk it out.

Later that same evening we had dinner together and got along well, exchanging stories about our boyhood.

Some time after that I had a similar problem of people "stealing Hugh Glass ideas" from me: one was a magazine writer who just simply lifted whole lines and paragraphs from my book, word for word. The other was a movie producer who took background material that I'd worked up by research as well as my new interpretation of certain acts of Hugh Glass. It would have been okay had he stuck to historical sources, as I had. While my brush with his studio was going on, Neihardt's daughter Hilda told me that if I sued, she'd like to have her father join suit with me. But I decided I had more to lose than gain, so we never did join forces against the Hollywood moguls.

I next saw John G. Neihardt in October of 1971, in Red Cloud, Nebraska, when he was given an honorary life membership and Distinguished Achievement Award by the Western Literature Association. He gave a fine acceptance speech and was his usual peppery self. We had several good talks and once even managed to sit by ourselves in a corner. Neihardt liked to tease and once, with a short laugh, wondered out loud why we should want to know each other. We should be interested in other people, not writers, from whom we could draw material. It wasn't good for writers to feed off each other.

I countered by saying we didn't see each other all that often that we might affect each other. Furthermore, I said that meeting him and seeing how he held himself, in fine mannered pride, was an inspiration to a younger brother writer. "You were the first to go into those Western American darks."

So he was. He was the first white writer living west of the Mississippi to celebrate our frontier, to make epics of our American experience.

In the summer of 1979, the University of Nebraska Press asked me to read a new edition of *Black Elk Speaks* they were going to publish. So finally I sat down and read the book carefully, in detail, to make up for not having done so before. When I finished, this is what I wrote to Nebraska:

I was glad you inquired if I'd like to read this new edition. This past week every evening I read it like a Bible, since that's what it really is. Except that it is our first American Bible, one that has come out of a place which chose its own people to be its spokesmen. I found it to be a gripping book, fascinating. Each evening I looked forward to reading a few more chapters. It became the centerpiece of my evening devotions in worship of this my own native land. I've loved this part of the country ever since I was born; and now having read *Black Elk Speaks*, "this place" has become even more sacred to me. It reconfirmed what I've always felt — that the past before my time and the present of my time are connected and are all of a piece. In fact *Black Elk Speaks* is one of the first books of stature to have arisen out of our American soil. *Ishi* comes close to it. But *Ishi* is not a Bible, where *Black Elk Speaks* is. No wonder Jung thought highly of it.

—Frederick Manfred

The Enduring Presence of John Neihardt

Bobby Bridger

IN 1965, AS A YOUNG MAN exploring the world of which I was then becoming aware, I discovered the work of the epic poet John G. Neihardt. As a songwriter and recording artist, I was doing research for my own epic ballads and the question arose in my mind whether or not there were any recorded songs of the mountain men.

One day I encountered Neihardt's masterpiece, *A Cycle of the West*. My thinking was soon consumed with images of Jed Smith, Hugh Glass, Major Henry, and others who people the epic poem cycle. History leaped from the pages of the *Songs*, and I realized that if there were not preserved versions of songs that the mountain men might have sung as they traversed the lonely Rocky Mountain streams, *A Cycle of the West* was certainly a powerful facsimile. The more I thought about it the more determined I became to find a way to translate these powerful songs into actual music. The result, I am happy to relate, has been the composing of *A Ballad of the West*.

My path eventually led to the John G. Neihardt Foundation in Neihardt's home town of Bancroft, Nebraska, where I learned many things about him that only can be gleaned from people who knew, loved and understood him. The foundation asked me to perform my hour-long ballad at one of its annual summer celebrations. I was delighted to perform for the people who gathered that summer; it was one of the greatest thrills of my career. Neihardt had become my

Bobby Bridger, singer, composer, and actor, appeared in the 1984 American Indian Theatre production of *Black Elk Speaks*.

guiding light and constant source of spiritual and poetic inspiration. My solitary comfort, in those difficult days for a struggling musician, was to remember what Black Elk had said of him:

> He is a word sender. This world is like a garden. Over this garden go his words like rain and where they fall they leave it a little greener. And when his words have passed, the memory of them shall stand long in the west like a flaming rainbow.[1]

I wanted to be, like Neihardt, a word-sender.

Nebraska was very hot and humid that August of 1979 when I arrived in Bancroft, but the sweet corn was coming in, and the people were the most open and kind I had met in my travels. Most of them had known Neihardt personally and quite a few of them had been his neighbors. After fourteen years of research, I was finally in the heart of John Neihardt's country, meeting his children and grandchildren, sitting in his study and reading his hand-written text of *A Cycle of the West*. Most importantly, however, I discovered the Lakota Prayer Garden that Neihardt and Black Elk had conceived and created on the grounds of the Neihardt Foundation. The garden is a hedge planted and shaped in a perfect circle. In the center of the circle where concrete red and black walkways cross, a small tree grows. The four quarters are represented by small flower gardens that grow just outside the circle. The night before my performance I slept in a borrowed buffalo hide robe in the center of the Hoop of the World under the Flowering Tree. There in the garden I prayed that I would approach the experience in a sacred manner, as Black Elk and Neihardt would have done, and take from it only to give back to the people in the highest and best possible way.

The next day before my performance I was introduced to a Lakota medicine man named Three Eagles. Very quickly he announced that he was only there as a messenger of the Great Spirit and to condone or condemn. The message that Three Eagles brought, however, was that the beautiful, circular prayer garden was offensive to the Great Spirit. I asked why, and he explained that the prayer garden was an ancient, important religious symbol to the Lakota people, and here

---

[1]*The Kansas City Star*, November 10, 1952, cited in Lucile F. Aly, *John G. Neihardt: A Critical Biography* (Amsterdam: Rodopi N. V., 1977), p. 171.

the symbol was in the land of the Omahas, a traditional enemy of the Lakota. Even worse, Three Eagles continued, was the fact that Black Elk had shared his most intimate vision with Neihardt openly and freely. Black Elk, he felt, in telling John G. Neihardt about his vision, had given away the power which it had.

According to Three Eagles, all that remained at Bancroft was the spiritual desecration of an important Lakota religious symbol. I wanted to point out that Black Elk had asked Neihardt to save his vision for men, and that ancient enmities between the Lakota and the Omaha should surely be resolved by now.

Before I could ask any more questions or attempt to defend the symbolic garden according to my understanding of how it came to be, I was whisked away and introduced to the audience. So I was soon well into the performance of my hour-long ballad, *Seekers of the Fleece*, although, I admit, with no little trepidation that my life-long search for spiritual reality, which I believed had been so benignly confirmed by my wonderful sleep in the prayer garden the night before, was crumbling as I sang.

While I sang I occasionally noticed Three Eagles as he stared at me. Then, after about fifteen minutes, his glance and his entire composure changed. He looked up over the circular garden and maintained his stare in that same, fixed position for the remaining portion of the ballad. As soon as I could approach him after the performance, I asked him what he had seen. Three Eagles told me that as I had begun to sing, six thunderhawks had flown in from six directions and circled the prayer garden while I sang. But upon completion of the ballad they had flown away. I told him I thought the hawks' appearance was a sign from the Great Spirit, Black Elk, and Neihardt that what was in Bancroft was good. I reminded him that throughout *Black Elk Speaks*, Black Elk had wrestled with the dilemma of whether to keep the vision for himself or to let it go out to all men. Finally, when Black Elk had decided to share his vision, he selected John Neihardt to send the proper words.

Three Eagles said that perhaps I was right, but that he would have to think about it some more. He was, however, now more receptive to my arguments that maybe something good was happening at Bancroft in perpetuating a center where people could learn about both Black Elk and Neihardt — people who might otherwise never know of them.

The next day I left Bancroft and was back on the road again playing music in nightclubs, concert halls, and people's living rooms. I returned home to Texas that fall, but the memory of my experiences in Nebraska at the prayer garden and later when I was performing stayed with me and gave me additional strength. The road beckoned again in 1980, and I was looking forward to returning to the Bancroft Lakota Prayer Garden.

By August, when I rendezvoused with some friends at the Lincoln airport, I had covered more of the West than I had in any previous summer, and many miles lay ahead. I was tired and looking forward to the peaceful pace of Bancroft and the farming communities of northeastern Nebraska.

I had met a woman at the Kerrville Folk Festival in Texas who had done a sacred pipe fast with Lakota Holy Man Pete Catches-His-Enemy. I had been trying to meet Pete Catches for many years, and Merri Lu Park and I struck up an immediate friendship based on our mutual interest in Lakotas and in Pete in particular. Merri Lu had just been visiting Pete during the Sun Dance at Pine Ridge and, remembering my invitation to attend the Neihardt Day celebrations in Bancroft, came down to join in the festivities.

Something important happened at the Fifteenth Annual Neihardt Day Celebration: there were as many young people as there were old people. The event had previously been a time when older friends and neighbors of Neihardt had gathered together, but these young people seemed to be searching for spiritual answers to critical questions: Who were they? What could they become? My traveling companion, Gene Arrington, and Merri Lu Park seemed to be representative of a troubled generation of young non-Indians. One could almost see a torch of understanding being passed from Neihardt to young people he had never met.

The speaker that year reminded us that exactly half a century ago Black Elk had asked Neihardt to return to talk with him when the grass was a certain height. He then spake of "two sensitive souls standing together probing the depths of understanding." He asked us to remember the Indian view of life in which community extends far

into the past and as far into the future, and said that wherever we
went, we shared with Neihardt and Black Elk the need to find the
meaning to our vision. With this good counsel in our minds, and
after a hearty meal only Nebraska people can prepare, my friends
and I packed our station wagon and began the trip westward across
northern Nebraska to meet with another traveling companion in
Sheridan, Wyoming.

I was excited at the opportunity to travel through so much ancient
Lakota territory. Neihardt's *Cycle of the West*, set in this very land,
provided a historical/geographical guide for our trip. I asked Merri Lu
and Gene if we could read Neihardt's poetry aloud as we drove west,
and they agreed.

As I noticed the sandy hills that follow the Niobrara River on its
lazy journey through Nebraska, I smiled. Neihardt was very keenly
aware of how much the western rivers had contributed to its exploration and settlement. He had made the great rivers of the ancient
Lakota lands — the Missouri, the Powder, the Rosebud, the Platte,
the Musselshell, the Tongue, the Big Horn, and the Yellowstone —
more than wavering, uncertain lines on a map. They became, under
his skillful craftsmanship, the stages for an epic drama. We were
traveling along one of Neihardt's most cherished streams.

When it was my turn to drive I noticed the cruise control device.
As I experimented with the sensation of driving a car with a cruise
control, I watched the Great Plains roll underneath the hood of the
car. I wondered if perhaps the Indians' love affair with the horse and
the great buffalo herds wasn't similar to our love affair with the
automobile. Both buffalo and car are clearly visible sources of power,
though extremely vulnerable. This strength/vulnerability causes men
to cherish some things so deeply.

Power and vulnerability lead to thoughts of the finitude of life,
and Neihardt's words, spoken through the character of Spotted Tail,
broke through my consciousness:

> The longest summer ends
> And nothing stays forever. We are old.
> Can anger check the coming of the cold.
> When frosts begin men think of meat and wood

And how to make the days of winter good
With what the summer leaves them of its cheer.[2]

Although this passage is from *The Song of the Indian Wars*, it still filled an appropriate place in my reverie, because the heat of August always foretells the blustery cold of December.

Merri Lu told us of the great gathering we had missed in July when people came together in South Dakota for the first "Black Hills Alliance and International Survival Gathering." This meeting was a ten-day, outdoor conference organized by Lakota activists, some of whom had earlier been at Wounded Knee, and nuclear opponents and traditionally conservative white farmers and ranchers, all of whom were beginning to realize their mutual interests in maintaining the Black Hills in its present condition. But there were interests, energy interests, exploring and drilling for uranium, precious metals and whatever else they might discover, who threatened the Hills. More serious, continued thoughtless exploration and exploitation was threatening to destroy the water table which underlies western South Dakota and Nebraska.

So these people had gathered, and in coming together had, if but for the moment, become powerful. Russell Means had commented on the strange bedfellows gathering during that event, calling their new alliance of "cowboy and Indian" "a fist the corporations can never pull apart." As Merri Lu told us about Russell Means' speech and his apt image, my mind went back to another image: the feeble fist raised by a toothless, ancient squaw. Neihardt used it to describe the protest of the earth when Red Cloud announced his determination to fight and make war on "every living thing west of the Mississippi River."

Pine Ridge, a little reservation town in the middle of rolling prairie foothills of the Black Hills, seemed the same as the last time I had passed through it. Some places never even appear to change. As on all Indian reservations, here one sees the drunks, oblivious as drunks the world over are to the intangible, abstract and serious issues which concern their society. An air of desperation always hangs over most reservation towns. It enshrouds Pine Ridge.

[2]*Twilight of the Sioux* (Lincoln: University of Nebraska Press, 1971), p. 13.

We traveled to Pete Catches' home, only to find that he wasn't there. We had to move on, so we left his house and started over the well-worn ruts that meander across the prairie surrounding Pete's place. As we drove along I looked across the prairie and saw a circular arbor, and in its middle a forked cottonwood pole still decorated with ribbons from the Sun Dance a few days earlier. It reminded me of the famous summer a half-century before when John Neihardt and those old Lakota men sat out under a similar arbor and spoke of the long ago. Were there some words still left in those old circled poles that Neihardt might have missed or that the old men, long after Neihardt and his daughters had retired for the day, had left for future seekers of wisdom?

Seeing the sacred tree brought an old thought back into my mind. I wondered again, as I had so many times in the past, if the Lakota weren't just waiting us out, as one might cringe temporarily before the onslaught of a storm, or as the Ashley expedition had once crouched along the Musselshell waiting for the blizzard to ease. The ancient Sun Dance held them together still, and beneath the poverty and despair there was a surging source of hidden energy which seemed capable of regenerating them quickly when the time came. Perhaps, I thought, they would outlast the invasion of the crazy white man. There was still a flickering eternal flame here which could not be extinguished, and maybe this flame also burned at Bancroft and in the hearts of those young people who had attended the festivities a week earlier.

Soon we gave up our search for Pete Catches-His-Enemy and moved towards the Black Hills and Wyoming. As South Dakota slipped behind us, Merri Lu and Gene seemed to be looking at the landscape differently. Reading Neihardt's *Cycle of the West* aloud as we traveled through the ancient Lakota heartland, they were both beginning to put land and history together. We stopped near the site of the Fetterman fight in the eastern foothills of the Bighorn Mountains and I read aloud as we looked over the scene:

> The hillsides bellowed with a surf of men
> Flung crowding on the boulders. 'Twas the end.
> Some trooper's wolfhound, mourning for his friend,
> Loped forward, pausing now and then to cry

His urgent question to the hostile sky
That spat a stinging frost. And someone said:
"Let yonder dog bear tidings of the dead
To make the white man tremble over there."
"No, teach them that we do not even spare
Their dogs!" another said. An arrow sang
Shrill to the mark. The wolfhound yelped and sprang
Snapped at the feather and was still.

(*Twilight of the Sioux*, p. 57)

Gene asked me about the Fetterman fight. Red Cloud had thought
that the fight with the white man would be over after he defeated the
soldiers so soundly. The Lakotas had won a major victory which they
thought would turn back the invasion of their lands. They could not
know that life was held so cheaply by the white man that the government would send troops to fight them until they were finally defeated.

Soon we were on the outskirts of Sheridan, Wyoming, and I was
anticipating a visit to the site of the Custer fight at Crow Agency,
Montana. Gene interrupted my thoughts with the observation that he
would never be the same after this trip. It is one thing to read poetry
in the comfort of your study on a cold winter night, and quite another
to stand with the prairie wind whipping your hair on the very ground
where something important has happened — standing right on the
bodies of the people who had made this an important spot, the flesh
long since decayed, but the atoms and energies of those bodies a part
of the very dirt under your feet. One old Crow chief, asked where his
land was, replied that it was under about eighteen inches of dust of
his grandfathers' bones.

Merri Lu had traveled the High Plains before, and knew the country well. But Neihardt's words had shaken her deeply also and she
was feeling pretty much the same as Gene. The spirit of the Lakota
was singing clearly in Neihardt's poetry and the meter created a
heartbeat as alive as the land around us. We rode into Sheridan
and met our friend Doug Krug before continuing our trip north
into Canada.

Dawn found us hurrying through the golden August wheatfields
of Montana, the Little Big Horn country. High and mysterious, these
plains were witness to the Custer battle, the final great statement of
the warriors of an ancient order. Maybe the Six Grandfathers had

given them that final pulsing, glorious victory in the afternoon June sun as an acknowledgment of the passing of the time of warriors.

The hilltop was shining orange in the morning sun as we drove to the visitor center. I carried my volume of *The Twilight of the Sioux* up the hill with me.

> The long line stormed upon the Hunkpapas
> Strung thin across the open flat. They fled
> Like feeble ghosts of men already dead
> Beneath those hoofs; for now it seemed they saw
> The yellow-headed Wolf of Washita
> Already on their heels with all his pack
> Potential in the dust cloud at his back,
> A howling fury!
>   Flame along a slough
> Before a howling wind, the terror grew
> As momently increased the flying mass,
> For all the others running up were grass
> Before that flame; till we became aware
> O how another voice was booming there
> Outsoaring Panic's, smashing through the brawl
> Of hoofs and wind and rifles.
>
>   It was Gall.
>   (p. 141)

I read the poem with all the excitement it had always evoked for me:

> Then broke a flying area of awe
> Across the rabble like a patch of sun
> Upon the troubled corn when gray clouds run
> And in the midst a glowing rift is blown.
> Pressed back before the plunging white-faced roan
> Of Crazy Horse, men brightened. How they knew
> That lean, swift fighting-spirit of the Sioux,
> The wizard eyes, the haggard face and thin,
> Transfigured by a burning from within
> Despite the sweat-streaked paint and battle grime!
> Old men would ponder in the wane of time
> That lifting vision and alluring cry:
> *"There never was a better day to die!*
> *Come on, Dakotas! Cowards to the rear."*
>   (p. 147)

Standing on the hillside I could see the troopers heading up the hill, and I was lost again in the swirling drama. Time itself stood still, and I shared that special grace which sacred places give to those who breathe the spirit of their mystery.

A voice called; Gene and Doug were calling out that we had stayed too long and had to get back on the road. We resumed our journey north towards Canada. I sat in the back seat and thought about Red Cloud, who had said, "The white man only made me one promise that he kept. He promised to take my land, and he took it."[3]

Soon in Canada I was again immersed in the life of a musician. Only occasionally did I return to read from *A Cycle of the West*. I guess it was the land; it was different. I wanted to wait until we returned to the Powder River country. Neihardt, Bancroft, Pete Catches, the Sioux — everything was far away while we were in Canada. But soon we were heading back down through the beautiful Canadian Rockies; once we were in the United States and approaching the Powder River, Neihardt and the Sioux returned to mind.

We were in a hurry now, rushing to the Crow Reservation for the world-famous Crow Fair. Billed as the largest gathering of Indians in the world, it has been known to attract thousands of Indians and up to 5,000 tepees. I have many Indian friends who go to Crow Fair every year and I was looking forward to seeing them and dancing. The festival of feathers, bells, and fancy dancers had attracted a colorful gathering of people to trade goods, tell stories, hold family reunions, and, most importantly, to dance. Indians from every tribe in the nation seemed to be represented there.

My old friend, Timberjack Joe, the mountain man, was there. Timberjack is a regular at most of the rendezvous and pow-wows in this region and I was delighted to see him again. He knew almost all the Indians in the world and had introduced me to most of them at one time or another during our many travels together. At his tepee I had a place to center my activities during the fair. My traveling companions left me with Timberjack, and I helped him put the lodge poles together and form the tripod into the cone-shaped frame of the tepee. As I struggled with the poles a small boy came up to me and

[3]Dee Brown, *Bury My Heart at Wounded Knee* (New York: Holt, Rinehart & Winston, 1970), p. 449.

offered his help. We talked and he explained that his father was Sioux and his mother Crow and consequently he spoke both languages. We finished setting up the tepee as the sun was going down, went inside and sat down, and Jay started to explain a few Crow and Lakota words to me.

That night was the first time I heard the criers. The Crow had appointed singers to travel around the festival grounds at regular intervals to sing songs of the event. Jay told me they were singing: "A dance! A dance! We all have come for a dance!" Somewhere in the midst of the criers' songs and my lessons in Crow and Lakota I fell asleep.

The next morning I was awakened to an old familiar voice echoing over the loud-speaker. It was Godfrey Broken Rope, the Lakota preacher and painter. A born-again Christian for many years, Godfrey had made his name as a painter and a preacher and everyone in the northern plains knew him and his voice. Several years before I had spent many hours talking with Godfrey, and I was anxious to see him again and hear the stories that had accumulated since we had been together. As usual, it took a while to get him to talk about anything except Jesus. Broken Rope has a sign on his easel that says: "I do not speak the white man's lingo unless you want to buy a painting or talk about Jesus Christ."

Godfrey usually has a tape recorder playing hymns softly in the background when you visit him. As we talked he called the old Lakota religion a good horse but a dead one — "Respect him, but don't ride." Maybe, I thought, but a generation of young people, Indian and white, is searching hard for a spark of life in that good horse. Maybe now we can learn to understand the interdependence of the universe.

My new friends from Texas had never slept in a tepee, and they were excited about the prospect of spending their last night at Crow Fair with Timberjack and me. We sat in a circle with some of my young Indian friends and talked. Suddenly we realized that we'd been talking so long that the last dance was escaping us. So we hurried to the great circular arbor, where one group of singers was still chanting for three lone dancers. My Texan friends had wanted to dance at least once at Crow Fair but now it looked as if they would not get the chance. We all knew not to intrude on strangers in the wee hours of the morning at *any* kind of dance. So we gathered around the singers and listened and watched as they sang and beat on their drum. Then an old, bow-legged man, his legs permanently shaped to the form of the many ponies he had ridden, danced up to one of the Texans and started showing him the basic steps of the Round Dance. Soon the two were dancing to the beat of the drum and the ancient songs of the Lakota singers.

I remembered the very first time I had attended an Indian pow-wow. Timberjack and I had come to dance and, since we were the only whites, I was scared to death. I did not want to offend anyone, and yet I knew that I wanted to dance and feel like I was a part of the group. Finally, after my third attempt, an old man danced up to me and had said, "This is good exercise. You will sleep good tonight." He introduced himself to me as Jake White Plume, a Northern Arapaho, and we quickly became friends. The man who danced with my new friend looked so familiar that I had to walk up to him and ask who he was. I could hardly make out his features in the dark, but I asked if he was a Northern Arapaho and he said that he was. I asked if he knew Jake White Plume and he answered, "I'd better know him, 'cause I am him." I had never seen Jake without his fancy dancer costume and I didn't recognize him in street clothes. He pulled off his baseball cap to show me a long, plaited strand of hair.

Jake and I visited for a while, and then I sat alone in the circular arbor where so many moccasins had danced over the years, and I remembered the sacred Lakota Prayer Garden in Bancroft. I offered a prayer to the Great Spirit for people like Jake White Plume, Timberjack Joe, Godfrey Broken Rope, and John Neihardt — every older person who mets a happy, young, open mind and ready heart and helps it become full with meaning. And I prayed for more heads and hearts and minds like theirs to teach us.

Off in the distance I heard a sound. For a minute it sounded like an old woman crying, but I soon recognized it as the sound of big trucks far out on the highway. No doubt they were loaded with heavy equipment headed to the Powder River and Little Big Horn coal and oil fields. Then I heard another stronger, higher whining. The Crow Fair criers rode through the night singing of the great event. I knew that the mechanical sound of "progress" will always be surpassed by that more ancient sound of people calling each other to dance and celebrate. And like those criers and John Neihardt who had filled my life with such meaning and purpose, I wanted to be a true sender of words.

Neihardt's Journey on the Missouri

Helen Stauffer

JOHN G. NEIHARDT'S *The River and I* is an account of his journey down the Missouri River in 1908. A travelogue, as the fifty photographs included in the book testify, it is much more than a pleasant chronicle of adventure at the turn of the century before interstate highways and airplanes. His work reaches back in American literature to the philosophical musings of Henry Thoreau in his *A Week on the Concord and Merrimack Rivers* and prefigures a number of later works such as the romance and high adventure of Richard Halliburton and the oral traditions retold by John Graves in his *Goodbye to A River*, a link in the nature writing genre of America.

The book is of interest on other levels than that of travel and adventure; it reveals much about Neihardt himself as a philosopher-poet-storyteller. Until one considers all three aspects of his writing, the style may seem inconsistent, ranging from the baroque to the arcane, to the modern reader removed some seventy years from its writing. Neihardt constantly juxtaposes the three aspects of himself — philosopher, poet and storyteller — in his story, often moving abruptly from the ridiculous to the sublime and vice versa, and shifting from exalted imagination or reverie to friendly conversation and reflection. His purpose is expressed at intervals in the book and

Helen Stauffer is a professor of English at Kearney State College in Nebraska and has specialized in the areas of western American literature and women's literature.

particularly in the title itself: *The River and I* is not just about the Missouri River, but about the river and Neihardt.

"In 1908," Neihardt tells us on the back of the 1968 edition of his book, "Casper Whitney, then editor of *Outing Magazine*, sent me down the Missouri River to write a series of articles for his magazine." The articles were later collected and published, together with fifty photographs, as a book that provided a great adventure story. Neihardt, twenty-seven in 1908, had already achieved a national reputation as a poet, short story writer, and essayist. He had edited a country newspaper for several years and published many short stories, usually based on the fur trapping period of the American West or the life of the Plains Indians in their traditional setting before the coming of the white man. Neihardt had published in the popular magazines of the day, *Overland, Outing, The Smart Set,* and the *American* magazine.[1] In 1907, several of his stories were published in a book titled *The Lonesome Trail.* That same year the Outing Company brought out his book of lyric poetry, *A Bundle of Myrrh.* The *Outing Magazine* editor knew Neihardt and his work well.

In addition to being an author and newspaperman, Neihardt qualified for the demanding physical requirements of the trip as an outdoorsman and physical fitness advocate. He was strong and agile, despite being only five feet tall: "hardly as tall . . . as Alexander," he commented.[2] (Alexander was reputed to be five feet-three inches.) A strong swimmer and proficient wrestler, he had a chest expansion of ten inches, which was considerable for a man of his stature. An inveterate hiker, he walked hundreds of miles and long after his Missouri adventure he continued to chop wood for exercise as well as for fuel.

Many people have a river in their lives. They define themselves by their relationship to that particular river. For Neihardt it was the Missouri, first, perhaps, because of his feeling for the sheer physical aspect of it. He related his first reaction to the Missouri when he saw

[1]Lucile F. Aly, *John G. Neihardt: A Critical Biography* (Amsterdam: Rodopi N.V., 1977), p. 34. I have used Dr. Aly's work extensively for background material on Neihardt's life.

[2]*The River and I* (Lincoln: University of Nebraska Press, 1968), p. 15. All further references are to this edition and are cited in the text.

it as a child of six. He was fascinated by its immensity and force: "I remember well the first time I looked upon my turbulent friend. . . . It was from a bluff at Kansas City. . . . The terror I felt made me reach up to the saving forefinger of my father. The river was in flood" (p. 2), and Neihardt watched "the demolition of a little town" as the waters surged through and over it. He saw the river as a "cruel, invulnerable, resistless giant that went roaring down the world with a huge uprooted oak tree in its mouth for a toothpick." He was frightened, but at the same time, "there was a dreadful fascination about it — the fascination of all huge and irresistible things. I had caught my first glimpse into the infinite" (p. 4).

Later he saw the river when the waters had receded; the water that had roared in the spring now only purred. Nevertheless, he was aware of its latent power, its dreadful economy of force. In winter, frozen over, it still carried the influence of a "tremendous personality" (p. 11). Back and forth over "this heavy sleeper" went the "pigmy wagons" of farmers, but when the ice broke up in the spring it was awesome: "The giant turned over, yawned and got to his feet . . . and went on singing, shouting, toward the sea." Since those early days Neihardt had become more closely acquainted with the Missouri: "I have felt the sinews of the old yellow giant tighten about my naked body . . . and we have become acquainted through battle" (p. 15).

The Missouri appealed to Neihardt through the physical senses and through the intellect and imagination as well. Over and over he stresses his fascination for its history, for, as he says, this was the route for the winning of the west — the road taken by the Indians before the coming of the white man, the road later taken by adventurers, trappers, hunters, and the "mountain men" who explored, mapped, and settled the west.

This great settlement of the west, in Neihardt's view, was far more significant than a local, regional or even national event. He saw it as one of the great archetypal movements in the history of the world, equating many episodes and those who acted in them with the great epics and heroes of the Greeks. "Perhaps never before in the history of the world has a river been the thoroughfare of a movement so tremendously epic in its human appeal, so vastly significant in its relation to the development of man," he commented (p. 20).

Neihardt was thoroughly grounded in the classics; he was especially fond of the Greeks whose literature and legends he knew well. Particularly in his first chapter. "The River of an Unwritten Epic," his introduction or apologia for making the trip, this affinity to epic literature is noticeable. He speaks of the vast northwest part of the continent in terms that suggest the beginning of the world, the creation, as told in the old stories: "Nature fashioned well the scenery for the great human story . . . she built her stage on a large scale . . . for the coming actors were to be big men, mighty travelers, intrepid fighters, laughers at time and space. . . . She left a vast tract unfinished, where still the building of the world goes on — a place of awe in which to feel the mighty Doer of Things at work" (pp. 20–21). He compares the Missouri to the Simois of Virgil, and for Neihardt the Missouri is certainly the greater river. The word *epic* appears time and again in the beginning of the story. "And the vast plains of my native country are as a mystery scroll unrolled, scrawled with a cabalistic write of infinite things" (p. 2).

At time he addresses the problem of telling the river's story. He points out that time and genius have glorified the events of the Trojan War. But though events just as momentous took place here, he complained, we have no writers great enough to put them into proper form: "We have the facts — but we have not Homer" (p. 23). Throughout the book Neihardt bemoans this fact, and this early work clearly presages his later decision to write *A Cycle of the West.* "The history of the American fur trade alone makes the Trojan war look like a Punch and Judy show! and the Missouri River was the path of the conquerors" (p. 23). "I am more thrilled by the history of the Lewis and Clark expedition than by the tale of Jason. John Colter . . . is infinitely more heroic to me than Theseus. Alexander Harvey makes Aeneas look like a degenerate" (p. 24).

Neihardt speaks of themes later taken up and developed at some length in his epic songs and mentions the "fine old Greek sense of fate" which we can find interwoven in the epics of the West he later produced. There were hundreds of heroes in the history of the Missouri River, builders of the epic West. "Heroes of an unwritten epic! And their pathway to defeat and victory was the Missouri River!" (p. 29). This unsung heroism was Neihardt's theme, his major reason for taking the journey, "When one looks upon his own country as from a height of years, old tales lose something of their wonder for him. It is owing to this attitude that the prospect of descending the great river in a power canoe from the head of navigation gave me delight" (p. 31).

Neihardt was an unabashed hero-worshipper; his desire to come close to the great doers and their country gave the journey its major point of interest. He idolized certain individuals, and in addition he personified and idolized nature itself. The river was to him a great hero waiting to be experienced. In terms strongly reminiscent of Walt Whitman he speaks of that river as his friend, a big brother, a dare-devil boy-god that sinned giant sins, through an excess of strength, a virile creature, a Titan. At another time he calls it a half-starved lion, "the ropy main current like the lean, terrible muscles of its back" (p. 8). His favorite and most frequently used reference to the Missouri is: "the Missouri — my brother . . . the eternal Fighting Man" (p. 16). "It is the symbol of my own soul, which is, I surmise, not unlike other souls." Neihardt elaborated on this last statement, expressing as well here as anywhere in his lyric poetry his understanding of the cosmic plan:

> In it [the Missouri] I see flung before me all the stern world-old struggle become materialized. Here is the concrete representation of the earnest desire, the momentarily frustrated purpose, the beating at the bars, the breathless fighting of the half-whipped but never-to-be-conquered spirit, the sobbing of the window-broken runner, the anger, the madness, the laughter. And in it all the unwearying urge of a purpose, the unswerving belief in the peace of a far away ocean (p. 19).

Later in *The River and I*, when the canoe reaches the mouth of the Yellowstone, Neihardt redefines the river. The upper Missouri, he decided, is female. Where the Yellowstone comes in all is changed and the river is decidedly male. He concludes that the upper Missouri is the mother, the Yellowstone is the father of "the turbulent Titan" that he considers the true Missouri of his youth, the Missouri he saw at Kansas City: "All of the unique characteristics by which the Missouri River is known are given to it by the Yellowstone — its turbulence, its tawniness, its feline treachery, its giant caprices" (p. 261).

Neihardt characterizes the river as feminine two-thirds of the way through the book, when he has reached the confluence of the rivers and seen the various elements which compose the river in their true form. The female, in most of Neihardt's descriptions, is seldom present. Writing at a time when male and female roles were still clearly defined in the Victorian or, more accurately, Edwardian, pattern, Neihardt does not question the mores of his time. But he is not dominated completely by them either.

One way, in this society, to prove one's manhood was to go on a safari; Theodore Roosevelt was one of Neihardt's favorite heroes. Roosevelt's favorite expression, "bully," occasionally surfaces in *The River and I*. During his actual voyage, few women appeared on the scene. That Neihardt lived in a family of women, that he liked women, and that in three months he would marry as a culmination of a story-book romance — none of these things are a part of the book. He does once or twice allude to the motherly type of woman whom he admires; otherwise his emphasis and admiration is reserved for "masculine" qualities: courage, strength, endurance, self-respect. His heroes are likened to those in the great *chansons de geste* and his romantic attitude toward the river falls into that category rather than that of a *chanson d'amour*. The old men on the docks at Kansas City who had traveled the river to Fort Benton and back "were such heroes! Great paw-like hands they had . . . eyes that had that way of looking through and far beyond things" (p. 61).

Neihardt envisioned the trappers who were around Fort Benton when it was active as "sturdy, rough-necked, hirsute fellows in buckskins... lean-bodied, capable fellows, with souls as lean as their bodies, survivors of long hard trails, men who could go far and eat little and never give up. I was very fond of that sort of man" (p. 65). And he remarked in admiration of his historic idols, "What males those cordelle men were — what stayers." And, speaking of a group of his contemporaries, in a passage straight out of Whitman: "Great, deep-chested, happy-looking, open air fellows, they were; big lovers, big haters, good laughers, eaters, drinkers — and every one of them potentially a fighting man" (p. 85). Yes, *The River and I* celebrates the maleness of the West as does his later *Cycle of the West*. Neihardt sees the West from a male point of view, but he sees it as a reflection of a pre-female saga, not as an anti-female story.

Thus Neihardt makes clear his role as the hero worshipper, the nature lover, the adventurer. But there are other facets of Neihardt to be found in this youthful book. His style, which ranges from the romantic to the facetious, from quietly contemplative to ebullient and effervescent, allows him ample opportunity for philosophy and reflection on the cosmic meaning of things. His philosophy may be expressed by far-ranging images or it may include homely aphorisms. One night, the beauty of the scene and, Neihardt recognizes and admits to himself, a satisfying meal sets the stage for speculation on man's place in the universe. Indeed, for Neihardt's place in the universe:

> "No now, no tomorrow, no yesterday, no I! Only eternity, one vast whole — sun-shot, star-sprent, love-filled, changeless . . . the swooning, half-voluptuous sense of awe and wonder, the rippling, shimmering, universal joy. And then suddenly and without shock — like the shifting of the wood smoke — the mood veered, and there was nothing but I. Space and eternity were I — vast projections of myself . . . the slowly revolving Milky Way was only a glory within me . . . and the deep, deep blue of the heavens was only the splendid color of my soul" (pp. 174–75).

He breaks this mood abruptly, as if a bit embarrassed: "Bill snored." His down-to-earth, often humorous philosophy is scattered throughout his more serious remarks: "True song is merely a hopeful condition of the soul. And so I am sure we sang very wonderfully that night" (p. 185), and "I love human nature, being myself possessed of so much of it" (p. 194).

Neihardt's style swings so far and so often that it can be contained logically only within the framework of direct communication — almost a one-to-one conversation rather than a written document. While he never resorts to "Dear Reader" phraseology, he often uses the informal conversational tone, addressing his reader directly: "Have you ever . . . ?" "You know . . ." "If you wish . . ." "Are you . . . ?" Exclamation points are everywhere and italics are used generously, and various slang expressions characteristic of that day are taken for granted. In addition to the enthusiastic "Bully!" Neihardt refers to his food as "grub," the train seats as "dusty plush." He calls the Indians "bucks" and "squaws," a terminology he would reject as an older and more sensitive writer. He talks of a man having a yellow streak. Ethnic slang of the day is included, though not stressed. He refers to a "Dago" and calls himself a "Dutchman," referring to his German extraction.

These devices are interwoven throughout *The River and I*, in that style so often used by newspapermen and local colorists of the early 1900's, a combination of hyperbole, understatement, heavy sarcasm and eternal cheerfulness characteristic of western writers like Twain and Bret Harte. Neihardt was particularly adept at using this, and his reflections on his experiences are often expressed in this rural, western style. Having experimented one evening with blue-crane soup, he notes that "the taste of that crane soup clung to me all day like the memory of an old sorrow dulled by time" (p. 208). About a haughty railway expressman who refused to help him hunt for a package he says: "I have since thought that he was the owner of the Northern Pacific system in disguise. I suggested that the personage might look about. The personage couldn't stoop to that; but a clerk . . . condescended to make a desultory search" (p. 296). At times he is even arch: "'Railroads,' explained I to myself, 'have a way of going somewhere; it is one of their peculiarities'." (p. 57).

But the style is skillfully crafted, allowing Neihardt to write beautiful, poetic passages without becoming maudlin or losing his audience. Almost always an elevated paragraph is juxtaposed with something very practical and down-to-earth. Just beginning the voyage, Neihardt waxes poetic about the morning, the sacred silence of the wilderness dawn, the fog, and the tang of wood smoke in a lonesome place. He associates himself with the "first man huddled close to the first flame, blooming like a mystic flower in the chill dawn of the world." He philosophizes that perhaps the primary purpose of such an outing is to strip one down to his essentials; he compares it with the "journey glorious" of life, associates himself with all men and the universe, and speculates on one's purpose in the world. He concludes the long musing with this reflection: "So strong was this thought in me when we cast off, that even the memory of Bill's amateurish pancakes couldn't keep back the whistle" (p. 134). This interspersing of factual discussion of the practical problems of getting from one spot to another with poetic or philosophic descriptions is characteristic of Neihardt's early experiment with style.

> In the lazy heat of the mounting sun, tempered by the cool river draught, the yellow sandstone bluffs, whimsically decorated with sparse patches of greenery, seemed to waver as though seen through shimmering silken gauze. And over it all was the hush of a dream, except when, in a spasmodic freshening of the breeze, the rude mast creaked and a sleepy watery murmur grew up for a moment at the wake.

> Now and then at a break in the bluffs where a little coulee entered the stream, the gray masses of the bullberry bushes lifted like smoke, and from them, flame-like, flashed the vivid scarlet of the berry-clusters, smiting the general dreaminess like a haughty cry of silence (p. 136).

The long, slow phrases, the alliteration — "break in the bluffs," "bullberry bushes," "flame-like flashed" — the descriptive words so carefully chosen, illustrate the poet in Neihardt. But in the following paragraph the words suddenly pick up momentum as we once more follow the actual movement of the canoe: "The Atom leaped forward, swung around a bend, raced with quartering wind, shot across another bend — and lay drifting in a golden calm" (p. 137). An unusual choice of words occurs here and there, again marking the poet: starsprent; mist-drift; gray-blue genius colored sky; dark brown tone of voice. But just as often Neihardt jolts the reader with: "Bill snored."

The journey down the Missouri did not go as planned. The original idea was that Neihardt, together with a photographer, identified only as Bill, and a young fifteen-year-old friend, The Kid, would travel in their carefully constructed engine-powered wooden canoe, christened the Atom, from Fort Benton, Montana, down the river to Sioux City, Iowa, a distance of some two thousand miles. Neihardt figured that once the canoe was built and the engine tested, they could make it down to Sioux City in ten days. Shortly afterwards, he revised his estimate to fifteen days as an accommodation to the unexpected events which might shape the trip. The trip took almost two months.

Numerous problems surfaced once they were embarked on this adventure. The most serious problem was the engine: fractious and undependable from the beginning, within a few days it gave out altogether. In an early upset of the canoe they lost a grub box and their paddles, and so they had to use some old, clumsily carved two-byfours. They lost their map, which was inaccurate anyway, and they could only speculate at times where they were. Another problem that continued to grow worse as the trip proceeded was the rapid falling of the Missouri River. The summer of 1908 was perhaps the most unfavorable time for a river trip in fifty years, Neihardt remarked. Devastating spring floods had suggested that the river would stay high late into the fall, but after inundating the country on all sides, destroying ranches and range land, the fickle and unpredictable river fell very swiftly. The canoe drew about 22 inches of water. As they went downstream, starting in July, the river dropped so swiftly that sand bars gave them endless problems, often requiring portaging, poling, or cordelling. The canoe itself became battered and worn, "a floating lump of discouragement" (p. 262).

In addition to the hazards and obstacles provided by the wild river, there were personal problems among the members of the expedition. Two drifters, who joined them with their skiff shortly after the start of the trip, became so depressed by the bad weather, the heavy headwinds, and the balky engine, that they left the group at the first opportunity. Although they had not been a part of the original group, their departure cast a depressing spell over the remaining members. Bill, the photographer, became homesick. Neihardt thought of him as "an expatriated turnip." When they reached the landing near the mouth of the Yellowstone, the first town in five hundred miles and a railroad point, Neihardt and The Kid shipped Bill home, along with all of their excess gear, "leaving all our impedimenta to be shipped by rail, that is, Bill, the tent, the extra blankets . . . everything but a few cooking utensils, an axe, a tarp, a pair of blankets" (p. 265). For the remainder of the voyage there would be just Neihardt and his young friend.

Fortunately Neihardt was able to trade off his worn wooden canoe and malfunctioning engine for a brand new metal canoe, hand-made, snug and sturdy. Naming it Atom II, he and The Kid continued paddling down the river. A second engine, ordered for delivery at Bismarck, did not arrive, giving rise to Neihardt's frustration with railroad clerks, and the two voyagers continued their trip downstream using their own muscle power.

The weather did not cooperate with the expedition. Again and again Neihardt notes cold, clouds, rain, heavy headwinds. Occasionally there was a day of beauty, color, and delightful scenery, but the weather was unusually bad and yet the water kept falling. In order to get to their destination before the river became impossibly low, they rowed sixteen to twenty hours a day and drifted down the river at night. At times they became stuck on sandbars because of poor navigation. They tended to fall asleep at night, which ensured them a certain amount of sandbar trouble, and once they awoke to find themselves running through a rapids, a frightening experience. Another time Neihardt, taking the paddle upon awakening, stroked upstream for half an hour before he discovered his mistake. The trip he thought might be a lark lasting less than three weeks took three times as long and most of it was accomplished by paddle or rowing, hardly what he had expected when estimating the duration of the trip.

Why did he stick with it? Neihardt himself questioned his motive: "Why didn't we quit? What is it all for? Well, what is life for? We were expressing ourselves out there on the windy river" (p. 303). *The Nation*'s reviewer called Neihardt a cheerful philosopher who "sees his world through rose-colored glasses."[3] He does sound cheerful about the difficulties and tribulations, so many more than he had expected on the trip. But there was an immensely practical reason for Neihardt's optimism; his audience would not have been interested in a tale of discouragement. But it was more than that. Neihardt's reaction to the vicissitudes only bears out his philosophy that endurance is a primary virtue. It was a challenge and Neihardt and his young friend met it with stubborn determination to succeed. The fact that others had quit only made it that much more imperative that the two remaining members finish the journey. The rewards were many. The land, the scenery was breathtaking. At times they felt as if they were the first men ever to see these vistas although they knew that others had been there before them, some thousands of years before them. They had solitude, nature, and time to think and meditate.

And, for Neihardt, there was the continual presence of history on the landscape. He stopped to locate the crumbled ruins of the old,

[3]*Nation*, XCI (December 8, 1910), 556.

important forts — Benton, Union, and others. He met Captain Grant
Marsh, who as captain of the riverboat *The Far West* had brought the
news of the Custer disaster to the outside world. He found the grave
of Sitting Bull and stopped to meditate on the fate of the old chief
and his people. Neihardt often stood in places where his heroes had
once stood: Hugh Glass, Mike Fink, LaVerendrye, Prince Maximillian,
Father DeSmet, the Gros Ventres, the Crow, the Blackfeet and
the Sioux.

The River and I was an interesting travel assignment, bringing the
Missouri River and its history to his audience. It was much more than
a writing assignment to Neihardt. This expedition was his great
archetypal journey to the American past, his homage to the exploits
and courage of previous generations of Americans. Although in
distance his trip might not compare favorably with that of the Argo,
or in duration with the travels of Odysseus, nevertheless this journey
was an important affirmation of Neihardt's poetic and intellectual
identity.

As Neihardt followed the paths of the great men of the West, he
could put them into his own historical/geographical perspective. He
knew then of their place, literally, through his own experiences, his
own reaction to that immensely powerful physical world of the West.
The fact that his journey lasted almost two months rather than the
short time originally contemplated proved ultimately rewarding to
him. The long days and nights battling headwinds and foul weather,
the long stretches of unoccupied and uncivilized country, the reliance
upon his own strength, courage and skill, his ability to withstand cold,
hunger, and discomfort, all these experiences brought him closer to
his frontier heroes in an authentic setting and gave him a reasonable
facsimile of their earlier experiences. He claimed a relationship with
them now that he had earned. "All about me would come and go the
ghosts of the mighty doers — who are my kin" (p. 32). He spoke
elsewhere of his praise for human ability to meet adversity, "I admire
[human nature] when it stands firmly upon its legs and I love it when
it wobbles. But when it gains power with increasing odds, grows big
with obstacles, I worship it" (p. 194).

Neihardt may well have been contemplating writing his *Cycle of
the West* before this journey. Certainly he had already felt the irresis-

tible fascination of the story of the western settlement. He obviously already had most of the necessary historical knowledge of the river, the land, and the events which had to have their Homer. And he had a strong sense that the writing should be done. But until he himself had actually traveled that river in this particular way, slowly and with difficulties unforeseen, until he had overcome them, he was not ready for his task. He says at the conclusion of *The River and I*: "When I started for the head of navigation a friend asked me what I expected to find on the trip. 'Some more of myself,' I answered" (p. 325). What he found was that he could now write the epic story of his country. That was his great discovery. His journey down the Missouri and his writing of it, made possible the later writing of *A Cycle of the West*.

Trappers and Indians—Neihardt's Short Stories

Lucile F. Aly

AMONG THE LEAST KNOWN WORKS of John G. Neihardt are the short stories that brought him his first literary reputation. He wrote them in the years before 1912, the same period in which he wrote his lyrics, when he was exploring techniques, experimenting with structures, and developing his style. After he abandoned short stories and lyrics for more massive works he continued to receive requests from editors for more stories, but complied only once, when he urgently needed money. The earliest stories were drawn from Neihardt's acquaintance with the Omaha Indians, whose reservation he visited in the course of his duties as assistant to a land-lease agent. His sympathy for the Indians, who were not aware that they were being defrauded of their lands, won him their acceptance, and colored the charming, vivid pictures he created of their life.

From wide reading of Western history Neihardt drew his tales of fur trappers, whose exploits in the rough fur country caught his imagination. Despite the uneven style of the stories, and the unmistakalbe signs of youthful effort, they deserve an audience for their own charm and for the extent to which they anticipate Neihardt's mature work. They were the kind of writing that introduced the West realistically into the mainstream of American literature.

Not all of the early stories were successful; Neihardt's one attempt

Lucile F. Aly is the author of *John Neihardt: A Critical Biography* and makes her home in Eugene, Oregon.

at sweet-scented romance, "The Face in the Balcony,"[1] can only be considered regrettable for its sentimental attempt to describe a sophisticated world Neihardt knew nothing about. It does not appear in either of the collections. "The Art of Hate,"[2] about two men who develop a mutual aversion on sight, and "Like a Woman,"[3] about a girl who saves her worthless lover from execution, contain impressive phrases, like the description of a fur trade manager as "a capital I swaggering in broadcloth," but both stories lurch into melodrama and claim for the characters emotions that are named but not motivated. "The Art of Hate" fails largely because Neihardt did not really understand hate; it was not in his experience. He once defined evil as "undeveloped good,"[4] and his hell, like Emerson's, had no devil.

As the stories progressed, Neihardt perfected his structural techniques and fine-honed his style. He developed frame formats with a narrator reminiscing, or an Indian directly addressing White Brothers and emphasizing the points they might find difficult. He learned to characterize through dialogue, to use stories within stories, sometimes to effect a surprise ending, sometimes to lend credulity by showing several people agreeing about an event. In a story about a Nebraska congressional election where the Indian vote was likely to be decisive, he used dialogue with great skill to show the flagrant manipulation of the unsuspecting Omahas. Frame structures that allow a narrator to clear up possibly misleading points by letting a listener ask questions or raise objections for the narrator to answer are especially useful in stories about different cultures, where misunderstandings can easily arise.

Neihardt's style also became more sophisticated in the stories. He developed in the Indian tales a flowing rhythm in the language that sounded much simpler than it really was, and at the same time suggested Indian idiom. Neihardt became adept at opening and closing stories effectively. "The Brutal Fact," for example, begins with the

[1]*The All-Story Magazine*, III (September–December 1905), pp. 343–350.

[2]*The American Magazine*, LXIII (April 1907), pp. 590–599; slightly revised in *The Lonesome Trail* (New York: The John Lane Company, 1907), pp. 93–109, and *Indian Tales and Others* (New York: The Macmillan Company, 1926), pp. 211–228.

[3]*The All-Story Magazine*, V (May–August 1906), pp. 179–183.

provocative sentence: "This is the tale of three men and a legacy not mentioned in the law books."[5] Another story also promises well in its opening sentence: "Here you have the story of the pigmy who would not fraternize with the Giant. It is an old one; indeed, it is the one story, often recurring, that makes the history of man tolerable reading."[6] Endings are often dramatic, as in "The Man Who Saw Spring," about a skipper of an icebound boat whose arrogance and panic caused the death of the entire crew. The final sentence describes what the rescuers found when they were able to reach the scene: "In a corner of the room a gray-haired man crouched and whimpered."[7] Some endings are cheerfully philosophical, as in "The Parable of the Sack," a morality tale about the love of money; in the final lines the storyteller answers the listener's question whether the story is true: "Yes, certainly it is true. For you must know, my friend, Truth does not happen — it exists!"[8]

Neihardt's Indian stories altered the focus on Indians in literature. The romantic Hiawatha/Last Mohican image of the noble savage, as well as the contradictory image of the war-painted fiend intent on torturing victims, had become entrenched in literature and in the American mind. But Neihardt knew real Indians. He liked the Omahas; he had camped on the reservation for weeks at a time, and as he said, had "sat in their lodges and tepees, eaten their meat, drunk their soup, smoked their pipes, and coddled their babies"; he found them pitiful, even when they were "for a moment majestic," for their culture was passing away. He was interested in them *not as Indians* but as people in a difficult and dispiriting situation not of their making — "human nature in the grip of fate, not Indian nature as a curiosity."[9] The Indian stories, set in the days before the white men swarmed over the prairies, bring the old times to life in Neihardt's descriptions

[4]*The Divine Enchantment* (New York: James T. White & Company, 1900), 1, 4, p. 46.

[5]*The American Magazine*, LXV, 5 (March 1908), p. 518.

[6]"The Epic-Minded Scot," *The Outing Magazine*, L, 11 (December 1908), p. 269.

[7]*The American Magazine*, LXV, 1 (November 1907), p. 55; also in *Indian Tales*, p. 306.

[8]*The Smart Set*, XXIV, 4 (April 1908), p. 124.

[9]Letter to Bob Davis, November 14, 1905.

of families going about their affairs, celebrating victory in dances, songs, and oratory, telling stories around the fire, meeting in council to decide when to hunt bison, whether to move the village, whether to take the war path. A prominent Indian writer, Susan La Flesche Picotte, daughter of the last Omaha chief, commended Neihardt for his accurate and sympathetic picture of Indians and his insight into their mysticism and spiritual beliefs.[10]

The themes of the stories fall into several patterns, with variations. Some stories deal with the misfit Indian — the small, weak, or misshapen in a society where physical prowess, bulk, and courage were essential to survival, therefore to the respect of peers. In "The End of the Dream," the story of Nu Zhunga, a bow-legged dwarf despised by the tribe for weakness, ridiculed for weeping over his dead pony after a battle, Neihardt stated the theme of the misfit stories: "The failure of the superstitious hope of an inhistoric savage is of as much importance to eternity as the calamitous miscarriage of a diplomat's scheme!"[11] As he said, he often "struck the minor chord" in the Indian tales;[12] they were written in the period when he himself felt lonely and unappreciated by his contemporaries, and he could sympathize with the Indian mood of helplessness and frustration. The tale of Little Wolf,[13] who was too small for a warrior, typifies the misfortunes of the handicapped. Angry at his disdainful treatment, he wraps himself in a wolf skin and tries to become a wolf. When marauding Otoes steal the squaws, including the girl he loves, Little Wolf goes after them, and tells the Otoes that the Omahas are coming. Seeing him still in the wolf skin, they think he is a talking wolf and flee in terror, but first they kill the women. The Omahas, arriving shortly thereafter, find the dead women and shoot Little Wolf for a real wolf; he was lying over the body of the girl. Occasionally the

[10]Editor's note to "The Look in the Face," *Munsey's* XXV, 4 (July 1906), p. 448, quotes from a letter to Dr. Picotte.

[11]*Overland Monthly,* XLVI, 3 (September 1905), p. 253. This story appears in *The Lonesome Trail* but the opening paragraphs including this quotation are not included.

[12]Letter to Bob Davis.

[13]*Overland Monthly,* XXXVIII, 6 (December, 1901), pp. 461–464; also in *The Lonesome Trail,* p. 194–203, retitled "The Beating of the War Drums."

misfit turns the tables, as in "The Smile of God,"[14] when an ugly little cripple, Shanugahi (Nettle), is driven out of the tribe, finds bison, and returns to save his people from starvation. He dies, but the story ends on a note of wonder, with two old men marvelling at being saved by a despised cripple.

The misfit Neihardt was best fitted to understand — the artist in an unappreciative world — is given full treatment in "The Singer of the Ache,"[15] with the warning at the outset that the story is about "One who walked not with his people, but with a dream," and is "not for anyone who has not followed the long trail of hunger and thirst that leads to no lodge upon the high places." Moon Walker, the Singer of the title, has a vision without the conventional bird, beast, or reptile to explain his assigned mission; his unorthodox vision of a woman's face cannot be interpreted, and repetitions of the vision-invoking vigil produce no better results. He composes songs; finally, to the bewilderment of the people, he leaves the tribe to travel through the world pursuing his vision, and returns at last to try to forget his dream. He retreats into his music with the sour disapproval of his neighbors, and is driven from the tribe. Ultimately, however, he "lived and was among all peoples" for "men sat down on dusty trails to sing his songs"; women sang them over fallen warriors and drew comfort from them. The old Omaha Neihardt uses as a story-teller spells out the theme: "Only they who have been fools are wise at last."

A group of stories revealing facets of the Omaha culture are based on the theme of rivalries and power struggles, but not for seats on the council that determined major policies; councillors were chosen by the wise elders, and only men of whom nobody could say anything evil were invited to join. Ambition struggles in the stories frequently concern medicine men, and tactics become ingeniously sinister. For example, the leading contender in the story appropriately titled "A Prairie Borgia,"[16] Wazhinger Saba, does not balk at endangering

[14]*Overland Monthly*, XXXIX (January 1902), pp. 544–547; also in *The Lonesome Trail*, pp. 219–228.

[15]*Watson's Magazine*, V–VI (October 1906), pp. 110–122; quotations, pp. 513, 515, 517. Also in *Indian Tales*, pp. 1–13 and *The Lonesome Trail*, pp. 110–122.

[16]*Overland Monthly*, XLII, 1 (January 1903), pp. 49–62.

the entire tribe by urging a move in the dead of winter to put his rival at a disadvantage — a move Neihardt pauses to label "insane." He calls the unfortunate young rival one of the "sacrificing men of genius" who become "incarnations of pity." He survives several attempts to remove him, but when Wazhinger Saba is able to procure from the river boatmen "something that will hurt much and kill," the Borgia triumphs by giving his young rival a fatal dose of arsenic. Afterward, he lives in terror, for the dying young man is able to pronounce a curse with his last breath. Another envious but less successful medicine man, Ebahamba, in "The Triumph of Seha,"[17] becomes incensed when his rival is able to bring rain; he invokes the rite of Wazhinada against Seha — a powerful ritual, in which the men go into their tents and think intensely and sternly of Seha. As a result of the thought pressure, Seha sickens but is restored, and the conclusion of the story invokes the miraculous. Seha changes himself into a fish; his enemy transforms to an eagle and catches him; Seha becomes a boulder, and the eagle crashes into it. Trumphant, Seha steps out of his rock and becomes a big man among his people; his enemy, according to rumor, skulks about with broken arms and a crushed face. An interesting feature of the Indian stories is the unperturbed fusion in the plots of down-to-earth, even canny, human nature and pure fantasy.

Sometimes Neihardt treated power struggles ironically, as in the tale of Little Weasel, who knew how to use his wits.[18] Banished for killing the rival who has stolen his feather, the proof of killing an enemy in battle, he starts a prairie fire. Returning in its wake, he claims to be loved by the fire spirits and quotes them as saying he has been punished by a foolish people. The Indians, as Neihardt says, "believing many strange things," feast him, and give him a new name, the Fire-Man. The story ends laconically, "and he was great among his people."[19]

[17]*Overland Monthly*, XXXVIII, 4 (October 1901), pp. 282–284; also in *The Lonesome Trail*, pp. 143–150.

[18]"Feather for Feather," *The All-Story Magazine*, III (September–December 1905), pp. 394–398. Also in *The Lonesome Trail*, pp. 45–57.

[19]*Overland Monthly*, XXXVIII, 5 (November 1901), pp. 355–357.

The theme of unselfish love and devotion runs through numerous stories, sometimes rising to heroism, as in "The Spirit of Crow Butte," when one brave remains on top of a butte holding off the enemy with gunfire while his comrades escape. In another such story the devotion of the maiden Umba to her hero, whose strongest regard is for his horse, prompts her to save his life, and later when he is slain in fighting, to kill his beloved horse so that its spirit may go with him.[20] A sadder version of the same theme is given in "The Fading of Shadow Flower,"[21] whose heroine pines and grows pale when her idol, Big Axe, is given an unwilling Ponca bride; the old people, noting Shadow Flower's decline, shake their heads and whisper that her soul has followed the summer, and her body is crying for her soul. Hovering about Big Axe's tepee, Shadow Flower looks through the flap and sees the Ponca wife kill Big Axe with a tomahawk, falter at killing the child, and flee. Shadow Flower gently takes up the baby, glides away, and is found on the prairie, dead, with the baby in her arms. The violence of the story is softened by the focus on Shadow Flower and her humble love; the old people say she has gone looking for Big Axe's soul, and the soberly matter-of-fact tone suggests a regretful acceptance of misfortunes.

Stories based on fur trappers, written when Neihardt was tooling up for his epic, deal with betrayal in diverse forms, justice and injustice, and survival, in an atmosphere heavily masculine. They are peopled with brawny men battling wilderness hardships — or each other — in quest of gold, furs, power, status, or victory in love. White women in the stories are remarkably passive; they reflect Neihardt's ingrained attitude about women, probably from his mother's teaching. Women were, in his words, "a great nation of people" to be respected and cherished. In his creed, a gentleman never mentioned a nice woman's name in a bar. It is therefore not surprising that the only women in the stories allowed passion or much initiative are Indians, half-breeds, or French. Neihardt liked women, and had many women friends, but he could not think of them except respectfully, and he sketches

[20]"The Singing of the Frogs," *Overland Monthly*, XXXVIII, 3 (September 1901), pp. 226–230.

[21]*Overland Monthly*, XLI, 2 (February 1903), pp. 145–150; also in *The Lonesome Trail*, pp. 75–92.

them lightly in his writings. The one exception, and the most fully developed female character in the stories, is the Paris prostitute Mignon[22] with whom Yellow Fox falls in love while on tour with Buffalo Bill's circus. Neihardt uses her to name a complex point, for Yellow Fox sees beyond the harlot to the essential woman in her, and gives her a new vision of herself. When he mistakenly takes over her household tasks to give her a life of ease, she rebels and is delighted at his angry reaction, for it enables her to demand the full woman's role. This story is perhaps a vindication of the little prostitute in one of Neihardt's lyrics, where he laments her deprivation of the fruitful wife-and-mother role. He protested vigorously his editor's objection to a prostitute in a respectable magazine story, and won his point;[23] he was already annoyed at the substitution in another of his stories of *darn* and *dern* for the authentic expletives he had put into the mouth of a salty character.

Neihardt recreates the atmosphere of the fur trade and gold-mining era with full regard for its vigor and brutality. "The Epic-Minded Scot," for example, gives an unvarnished view of the ruthless destruction of a trader reckless enough to defy the reigning Great Fur Company. In "The Parable of the Sack,"[24] an ugly facet of human nature at work appears in the callous defrauding of the gullible young greenhorn straight off the farm by a con man in a flashy suit, who sells the naive lad a salted gold mine. The greenhorn himself is described in terms that at once emphasize the callowness of the boy and convey sympathy for the sister and mother waiting in naive confidence back at the farm for their young wonder to return with a fortune.

In three stories Neihardt ventured into science fiction. They are not his most successful stories, perhaps because in each one he seems to shy away from fixing his purpose clearly. He had for some time been interested in psychic phenomena; he read widely on the subject, and was particularly impressed with Ouspensky's theories and F. W. H. Myers' discussion in *Human Personality and Its Survival of Bodily*

---

[22]"Mignon," *The Smart Set*, XXI, 3 (March 1907), pp. 55–60; also in *The Lonesome Trail*, pp. 239–254, and *Indian Tales*, pp. 88–103.

[23]Letter to Bob Davis, November 9, 1906.

[24]*The Smart Set*, XXIV, 4 (April 1908), pp. 116–124.

Death,[25] but the inconclusiveness of the stories suggests that he had some reservations about the implications. He was always a little reluctant to discuss the question unless he was sure of his audience. The stories are interesting, but they do not quite finish the idea. "The Ancient Memory,"[26] about John Smith, who after several drinks becomes Julian Spears, fur trader, also Red Slayer of the Nickaroos, and king of big men when Attila the Hun was ravaging Europe, suggests Neihardt's speculation that continuing consciousness crosses barriers of time. Although Neihardt gives Julian Spears a vocabulary and syntax beyond the reach of Smith, the point of the story is never really fixed. The tale "Beyond the Spectrum,"[27] somewhat less clearly deals with the crossing of time barriers through the account of the man Steel, who can vanish into other ages and return at will. The story includes in its personnel a white cat somewhat vaguely identified as Cleopatra, whose court Steel says he has visited. Again the point of the story is not perfectly clear. The story has overtones of Poe, not only in theme, but in style and syntax as well. A much surer grasp of his materials is clear in "The Red Roan Mare,"[28] Neihardt's last short story, about two cavalrymen in the Custer war, one a Celt, the other a sardonic Frenchman. The story features the return of a vengeful ghost, and both plot and characters recall the Fink–Carpenter story in Neihardt's epic, as if he were speculating about the outcome if the roles had been reversed. The French Bill marries the girl in this story, provoking the jealousy of Celtish Jim, and is fatally wounded in the Reno battle. Jim inherits Bill's handsome horse, falls in love with and marries his widow, and has strange experiences with the horse. He feels four hands in the gauntlets when he rides, and at last meets his death when the mare bolts with him into an arroyo full of waiting Sioux. The old cavalryman who recounts the story adds eerily that he saw two men in the saddle. Neihardt's careful marshalling of

[25] P. D. Ouspensky, *Tertium Organum*, (New York: Alfred A. Knopf, Inc., 1922); F. W. H. Myers, *Human Personality and Its Survival of Bodily Death*, (New York: Longmans, Green and Co., 1903), 2 vols.

[26] *The Smart Set*, XX (June 1907), pp. 98–104.

[27] *The Smart Set*, XXI (April 1907), pp. 48–58.

[28] *Indian Tales*, pp. 179–210.

details against a realistic, well-researched setting of a historic battle builds suspense and gives plausibility to an uncanny tale.

Some of Neihardt's best stories are based on the theme that two different cultures cannot fully understand each other. The gently ironic tale, "The Heart of a Woman,"[29] related by an Indian father and his daughter to the council sitting in judgment, describes the girl's love for a white man who had fled civilization, and her jealousy of his violin, the "singing spirit" he loves. The girl relates how she took care of the violin when the man went hunting, for his sake "washed it well that it might be clean and of a good smell," and was reprimanded for her pains. She bore the man a son and grieved when the father was not pleased; finally, convinced that the violin was the spirit of a white woman the man had loved, she gave way to jealousy and destroyed the violin with a knife. The council members ponder and shake their heads, asking each other who can understand the heart of a woman. By white men's laws, the woman might have been charged with the destruction of property and assessed the monetary value of the violin, but the Indians recognized a deeper, more serious crime in the destruction of something the white man loved. Baffled by so unusual a case, they take refuge in the impenetrability of the female mind. The regretful irony in the tone of the story seems to sigh over the inability of human beings to understand each other.

One of the most poignant stories, "The Last Thunder Song,"[30] conveys the pathos of a conquered race disillusioned in its own values. The story is set in 1900 at an annual Indian pow-wow, where an old medicine man performs a dance and sings a thunder song to bring rain. At the climax of the song, young Indians who have attended the Indian school and learned skepticism burst into laughter — "the audacious Present jeering at the Past, tottering with years." Afterwards the Mission Preacher seeks the old man out and tries to comfort him. The medicine man says bleakly, "God? He dead, guess." After further thought he adds wearily, "White God dead too, guess."

---

[29]*Tom Watson's Magazine*, V–VI(1906), pp. 55–58; also in *The Lonesome Trail*, pp. 229–238, and in *Indian Tales*, slightly revised and retitled "Vylin," pp. 78–87.

[30]*Overland Monthly*, XLIV, 4 (October 1904), pp. 341–436; also in *The Lonesome Trail*, pp. 276–287.

Neihardt's sentiments are clear in the irony he attaches to the three men who discuss the incident — the Preacher, who sees Indians as ruins of former glory; the physician, who finds them "pretty much like white men"; and the skeptical newspaperman. Neihardt saw the pathos of a destroyed faith and was none too sure the three moderns were right.

Another story, "The White Wakunda," originally titled "The Lonesome Trail,"[31] examines a further problem of race understanding, the Indian acquaintance with Christianity. Wa-Choo-bay, an Omaha given a strange vision of a mysterious canoe that bore him away on a river and an old man who taught him about thunder spirits so that he could summon rain, represents a Christ figure. The details of his life parallel the Christ story: he declines to take a wife, leaves the tribe and returns to teach them about the "great white medicine man" and his message of peace and kindness to enemies. He is rejected when he cannot perform medicine-deeds nor stop a smallpox epidemic. He is lashed to a post, whipped to death, and mourned by a woman he has renamed Mary and a wolf he befriended. This story, written some twenty-five years before *Black Elk Speaks* and *The Messiah*, foreshadows the later works, and might also be said to sound echoes of Plato's parable of the philosopher who has seen the light of truth and tries to share it with his fellows.

"The Alien,"[32] considered by numerous critics and students of Neihardt to be his best story, concerns a brutal half-breed, rejected by father and family and unacquainted with kindness from anyone. Fleeing from justice, he takes refuge in a cave where he encounters an injured female wolf that attacks him, but feebly enough to be subdued. The wolf licks the wound she has made, and the man, responding to the first caress in his experience, names the wolf Susette and nurses her back to health. Inevitably, with restored strength Susette acquires an admirer of her own kind, and the man, jealous of a rival, tries to keep Susette from joining the pack. The male wolf

[31]*The All-Story Magazine*, IV (January–April 1906), pp. 274–280; also in *The Lonesome Trail*, pp. 123–142, and *Indian Tales*, pp. 29–48, titled "The White Wakunda."

[32]*Munsey's Magazine*, XXXVI, 5 (February 1907), pp. 706–712; also in *The Lonesome Trail*, pp. 11–30, and *Indian Tales*, pp. 116–135.

attacks him, and he is horrified when Susette leaps to the attack also. Starkly effective in its clashing of raw emotions, the story says firmly that if a man rejects the values of civilization and chooses the savage world, he cannot transfer civilized values to that world, however urgently he may find he needs them. It is also a sobering study of an abused person unable to find a place in the world that produced him. The story has been compared to Balzac's "A Passion in the Desert," and was highly praised at the time of its publication. In Neihardt's original version Susette produced pups, and the man suffered intense jealousy, but the editor protested the pups as putting too severe a strain on the sensibilities of *Munsey's* readers, and Neihardt reluctantly deleted them.[33]

To students of Neihardt's work, one of the fascinating aspects of the short stories is the extent to which they anticipate his later work. He may have believed the critic who wrote that in them he had "material for a dozen novelists,"[34] for two of his novels are compilations of stories. *The Dawn Builder* compounds "The Discarded Fetish,"[35] a genial, down-to-earth, folksy story, and a fantasy like "Beyond the Spectrum," though the spectrum of seven colors is transposed to a seven-note chord. It also incorporates the iced-in boat theme of "The Man Who Saw Spring." The fusion is not successful, chiefly because the original stories represent totally different and incompatible moods. "The Discarded Fetish" itself is an excellent story, one of Neihardt's best, about a good-humored, homely boatman with one eye and a wooden leg, his friendship with a young boy, and his diffident love for the boy's mother, an attractive widow. He sets up a profitable saloon with liquor salvaged from a sunken boat, and leaves the business to the boy when he departs from the town after the "widow's" husband turns up unexpectedly. The tone of the story is both humorous and rueful. The main character, Mr. Waters, with his easy-going philosophy of good will and unassuming cheerfulness, kindles in the reader hope for the human race. Neihardt's story caught

[33]Letter to Bob Davis, November 9, 1906.

[34]Review of *The Lonesome Trail* in the *Saturday Review*, CIV (September 21, 1907), p. 2708.

[35]*The Dawn-Builder* (New York and London: Mitchell Kennerly, 1911); "The Discarded Fetish: A Romance of the Missouri," *The Smart Set*, XXII, 3 (July 1907), pp. 116–140.

the attention of a theatrical producer, who wanted to turn it into a play for the Broadway stage, but the plans ultimately fell through.

Life's Lure, Neihardt's second novel, was quite clearly produced from the interweaving of two stories. "The Lure of Woman,"[36] the tale of a gambler appropriately named Devlin, who ruins a young man financially, seduces his wife, and corrupts everyone possible, and "The Parable of the Sack" conjoin with less discernible seaming than that of the first novel, but the story does not quite ring true. The characters are not fully credible, and the theatrical style is overloaded with cliché.

Germs of Neihardt's epic, *A Cycle of the West* are frequent in the short stories. The entire plot of *The Song of Three Friends* is sketched in "The Brutal Fact," and the characters are the same Celt, Saxon, and Frenchman. Neihardt had obviously worked out his ending of the story as early as 1908, although the *Song* was not begun until February 1916. The prairie fire featured in the story was described in "The Nemesis of the Deuces,"[37] with some of the same metaphors and phrases of the *Song*, such as the "giant gaudy flowers" blooming and falling. Forecasts of *The Song of The Messiah* can be traced to several stories. In "The Ancient Memory" Julian Spears dreamed of being the Red Slayer, Messiah for his people, and also of a terrible battle of the Sioux. In "The Epic-Minded Scot" McDonald tries to use the Messiah rumor for his own ends and convinces himself he is the man to lead the Sioux against the white man; he dies a dreadful death when the Indians realize he has deceived them, for the dead do not rise as he has promised to come to their aid.

Neihardt's stories reveal his youth, but they also reveal his artistic promise. The firm, flowing style and solid narrative techniques with which he related Indian legends in his last novel, *When The Tree Flowered*,[38] had their beginnings in the early short stories. As Henry Holt said, he had "talent to burn."

---

[36]*Life's Lure* (New York: Mitchell Kennerly, 1914); "The Lure of Woman," *The Smart Set*, XXIV, 2 (February 1908), pp. 150–160.

[37]*The American Magazine*, LXIV, 1 (May 1907), pp. 88–99 (originally titled "Nemesis"); also in *The Lonesome Trail*, pp. 288–303, and *Indian Tales*, pp. 258–274.

[38]New York: The Macmillan Company, 1952.

Neihardt and the Western Landscape

Vine Deloria, Jr.

THE NAME OF JOHN G. NEIHARDT invokes visions of the Lakota holy man Black Elk, of the rugged mountain men of Henry's expedition, and of the raging Niobrara River, pouring its heart into the Missouri, itself rampaging down from the far reaches of Montana with its load of continental debris. Being human, we are interested in the story of our kind, the solitary men who tramped the wilderness seeking furs and freedom. We often fail to realize that they existed within a particular context, historically and geographically, and that their story is unique because the time and place were also unique. Too often we are caught up in the experiences of Neihardt's people and we fail to see the larger canvas upon which his stories take place. The western lands had their own story, not a geological story as James Michener often appends to his novels, but a personal and energetic story of life written on a cosmic scale. Fortunately for us, John Neihardt chose to tell as much of the story as he knew, and he pointed the way at times to a better understanding of what the western lands might tell us if we listen.

Neihardt was intimately involved in the western landscape his whole life. His early childhood was spent in a sod house in Illinois before the family moved to Nebraska. "If I write of hot-winds and grasshoppers, of prairie fires and blizzards, of dawns and noons and sunsets and nights, of brooding heat and thunderstorms in vast land,"

Vine Deloria, Jr., is an author, political commentator and Indian historian, who teaches in the Department of Political Science at the University of Arizona.

he wrote in his introduction to *The Mountain Men*, a 1948 edition of
the three *Songs* which compose Volume I of *A Cycle of the West*,
"I knew them early."[1] One cannot therefore simply take the Neihardt
epics as if they spoke of some abstract set of truths set apart from the
lives of people, particularly western people. Indeed, it is his close
relationship with the western lands that sets his *Songs* of the mountain men apart from other writing about the West.

Neihardt's *Cycle* is filled with autobiographical references to the
western lands, and by carefully tracing some of his experiences we can
locate a few instances where he works his own vivid perceptions of
his land into his poetry. It is particularly important to recognize this
interweaving of personal experience and historical saga because ultimately Neihardt suggests in his poetry such an intimate relationship
of men and nature that one becomes the other in a metaphysical sense.
That is to say, nature is used to describe the emotions of men and the
activities of men are used to describe the natural conditions of the
land. Only a person who has been tempered by the searing heat of a
Great Plains summer or chilled by a sudden blast of arctic air in
winter as the Plains give way to soul-numbing blizzards can write of
the intensity of the western lands and bring his epics to life in their
proper geographical setting.

In searching for Neihardt's understanding of the western lands one
is struck by the youthful naivete of *The River and I* in which he first
encounters the vastness of the northern Missouri break country. This
book, actually a well-edited series of articles for *Outing Magazine*
whose editor commissioned Neihardt to travel down the Missouri in
1908 — a time when there was still little settlement on the river in
Montana and North Dakota, displays his first reflections on the
western lands and their meaning to us. *The River and I* received warm
praise from critics who saw it as a delightful example of the loving
warmth which nature was capable of generating in a young man.
And Neihardt displays all the awkward enthusiasm of a young
writer trying desperately to make these lands come alive for his
eastern readers.

His language in this book is often ponderous and grandiose, as if
by invoking other images and concepts he can communicate the

[1]*The Mountain Men* (Lincoln: University of Nebraska Press, 1971), pp. viii–ix.

majesty of endless rolling plains and unmeasured miles of river breaks. Like other writers of landscape trying to bring their readers into focus with the land, Neihardt relies upon the commonality of religious experience. "I have seen the solemn rearing of a mountain peak that gave me a deep religious appreciation of my significance in the Grand Scheme," he writes, "as though I had heard and understood a parable from the holy lips of an Avatar. And the vast plains of my native country are as a mystic scroll unrolled, scrawled with a cabalistic writ of Infinite things."[2] It must have been a ponderous mountain to have called forth such sonorous phraseology, but the readers of *Outing Magazine* in the East must have been delighted with this kind of communication. It is ironic that Neihardt here attempted to create the same sense of religious mystery for which he was enthusiastically applauded in *Black Elk Speaks* half a century later.

The River and I provides us with the intellectual setting for Neihardt's epic songs in that it announces joyously that men are free to live heroic lives. Nature then becomes the gigantic stage upon which these lives take on heroic meaning. "We no longer write epics," Neihardt announces, "we live them." And, he continues, "We no longer prostrate ourselves before the immortal gods. We have long since discovered the divinity within ourselves, and so we have flung across the continents and the seas the visible epics of will" (p. 23). What typically American optimism! How representative is Neihardt of the age when Americans, having finally closed the frontier and won the West, now found meaning only in celebrating their victory and pretending that it wasn't all that difficult for such a race of hardy men. The year 1908 was, if we remember correctly, the time when Teddy Roosevelt stamped around America shouting "Bully" to indicate his pleasure at muscular achievement.

So the divinity of man gave fruition to Neihardt's perception that nature had provided a worthy arena in which a race of supermen, the American, could forge a drama more significant than the Greeks and Trojans in their legends. "The history of the American fur trade alone makes the Trojan War look like a Punch and Judy show! and the Missouri River was the path of the conquerors," he crowed. "We have the facts — but we have not Homer" (p. 23). And yet when

[2]*The River and I* (Lincoln: University of Nebraska Press, 1968), p. 2.

he looked deeply into his own soul he found there the Missouri River looking back at him. "But the Missouri is more than a sentiment — even more than an epic. It is the symbol of my own soul, which is, I surmise, not unlike other souls. In it I see flung before me all the stern old-world struggle become materialized. Here is the concrete representation of the earnest desire, the momentarily frustrated purpose, the beat at the bars, the breathless fighting of the half-whipped but never-to-be-conquered spirit . . ." (p. 19).

Looking for a Homer, and perhaps deciding within himself that by announcing this quest he had already identified the western Homer, Neihardt turned his attentions to the nature of the epic. "An epic story in its essence is the story of heroic men battling, aided or frustrated by the superhuman. And in the fur trade era there was no dearth of battling men, and the elements left no lack of superhuman obstacles" (p. 23). These two elements — human conflict and superhuman obstacles, seemed to the youthful Neihardt, filled with wonder that he was passing through lands trod earlier in the century by an archetypal group of Americans, to constitute the substance of American epic experience. It is significant, then, to note that his three major *Songs* dealing with the mountain men, *The Song of Three Friends*, *The Song of Hugh Glass* and *The Song of Jed Smith*, are almost precisely balanced with these two themes. *Three Friends* deals primarily with human conflict, *Hugh Glass* with superhuman obstacles, and *Jed Smith* synthesizes human conflict and natural obstacles.

We see two perceptions of landscape by Neihardt in *The River and I*, the heroic, ultra-historical dramatic perception and the practical realistic experienced perception. He looks at the drab and sere quality of the Missouri headlands and decides that

> . . . in the building of the continent Nature fashioned well the scenery for the great human story that was to be enacted here in the fulness of years. She built her stage on a large scale, taking no account of miles; for the coming actors were to be big men, mighty travelers, intrepid fighters, laughers at time and space (p. 20).

And he begins to juxtapose nature and human aspirations to find that existence in the western lands is essentially a test between two cosmic opponents — man and land. Rugged features are no longer simply landscape, nor do they have a tinge of homogeneity. Instead they are deserts for the trying of strong spirits; grotesque volcanic lands — dead, utterly ultra-human — where athletic souls might struggle with despair; impetuous streams with their rapids terrible as Scylla, where men might go down fighting; thus Nature built the stage and set the scenes (pp. 20–21).

Inspired by such thoughts, a writer, and particularly a poet, might march eagerly into the wilderness in search of heroic adventure. But after several hours of marching or boating along the endless Missouri breaks, one is humbled considerably by the vastness of the landscape. Neihardt learned quickly that although in the abstract the western lands were designed for dramatic events and superhuman personalities, they nevertheless had a power of their own which could not be denied and before which the human appeared small and confused. In his most honest practical moments he described the land more accurately:

> The monotony of the landscape was depressing. It seemed a thousand miles to the sunrise. The horizon was merely a blue haze — and the endless land was sere. The river ran for days with a succession of regularly occurring right-angled bends to the north and east . . . until at last we cried out against the tediousness of the oft-repeated story, wondering whether or not we were continually passing the same point, and somehow slipping back to pass it again (pp. 239–240).

Thus do epic poets count their blisters and bow before the grandeur of the western lands. But these lands, in turn, produce the kind of men that Neihardt knew had conquered them.

When we turn to the three *Songs*, if we have absorbed the message and experiences of *The River and I*, we discover familiar images and descriptions as if in making the voyage downstream Neihardt had transcended time and become a mountain man himself. Coming down river, Neihardt had encountered the Missouri winds which are funneled through breaks in the banks and achieve an incredible velocity. Neihardt passed Black Bluffs Rapids, the boat dipped into a placid, prolonged, lake-like section of the river. And then,

> At the next bend, where the river turned into the west, the great gale that had been roaring above us, suddenly struck us full in front. Sucking up river between the wall rocks on either side, its force was terrific. You tried to talk while facing it, and it took your breath away. In a few min-

utes, in spite of our efforts with the paddles, we lay pounding on the shallows of the opposite shore (pp. 137–38).

This personal experience is recapitulated in *The Song of Three Friends* in the section "To the Musselshell," and Neihardt, transposing the experience to a snowstorm, describes the same emotions and helplessness which he had felt:

> The windward reaches took their breath away
> Ghost-white and numb with cold, from bend to bend,
> Where transiently the wind became a friend
> To drive them south, they battled; till at last
> Around a jutting bluff they met a blast
> That choked as with a hand upon their throats
> The song they sang for courage; hurled their boats
> Against the farther shore and they them pinned (pp. 34–35).

Neihardt paid particular attention to the western weather as an indication of the energy of the landscape. His raw material was the endless plains bisected occasionally by streams and held together by the sinuous Missouri, which he understood in the dog days of summer as a "half-starved lion" with the "long dry bars . . . like the protruding ribs of the beast when the prey is scarce, and the ropy main current . . . like the lean, terrible muscles of its back."[3] Yet knowing its terrible potential, Neihardt faithfully reproduced the sudden gathering of strength in his description of its human perceptions of the land:

> Abruptly in a waning afternoon
> The hot wind ceased, as fallen in a swoon
> With its own heat. For hours the swinking crews
> Had bandied scarcely credible good news
> Of clouds across the dim northwestward plain;
> And they who offered wagers on the rain
> Found ready takers, though the gloomy rack
> With intermittant rumbling at its back,
> Had mounted slowly.[4]

Almost hiding from human perceptions of its intensity, the storm appeared so casually that the men gambled on whether or not it would

[3]*The River and I*, p. 8.
[4]*The Mountain Men, The Song of Three Friends*, pp. 25–26.

rain and "scarcely were the craft made fast to clumps of willow fore and aft, When with a roar the blinding fury rolled upon them; and the breath of it was cold."[5] In *The Song of Three Friends* we find this accurate portrayal of the western landscape but we do not find it providing superhuman obstacles. It remains a background on which the human drama is played out. Even during the prairie fire when Talbeau and Fink barely survive and Fink confesses his terrible secret — that he aimed to kill when shooting the cup off Carpenter's head, the human emotions are dominant.

In *The Song of Hugh Glass*, however, the landscape takes on an added active role in the story. Glass, left for dead after having been mauled by a mother grizzly bear, revives, and his thirst for vengeance fuels his desperate crawl back to Fort Kiowa on the Missouri. Faced with a technical problem of illustrating human emotions during the crawl, Neihardt merges human feelings and the particularities of land to provide us with some memorable images. Describing Hugh's tremendous effort to rise after coming to consciousness and realizing he has been abandoned, Neihardt reverses the image of nature and allows it to inform us of Hugh's physical condition:

> The painful effort spent
> Made the wide heavens billow as a tent
> Wind-struck, the shaken prairie sag and roll.
> Some moments with an effort at control
> He swayed, half raised upon his arms, until
> The dizzy cosmos righted, and was still (p. 155)..

Then Neihardt shifts quickly to a neutral nature as Glass ponders his fate:

> saw the non-committal sky,
> The prairie apathetic in a shroud
> The bland complacence of a vagrant cloud —
> World-wide connivance! Smilingly the sun
> Approved a land wherein such deeds were done;
> And careless breezes, like a troop of youth,
> Unawed before the presence of such truth,
> Went scampering amid the tousled brush (pp. 158).

[5]Ibid.

But this nature is not really neutral. Glass expects it to have formed some kind of moral judgment regarding the events that have transpired. His expectation that the land would have formulated an ethical posture regarding his situation indicates how closely Neihardt has tied human emotions and natural process.

As Glass commences his crawl, Neihardt uses the description of the landscape to indicate the human emotions, allowing nature to play the role of the human while the human becomes a passive, almost inert observer:

> All morning southward to the bare sky rim
> The rugged coulee zigzagged, mounting slow;
> And ever as it 'rose, the lean creek's flow
> Dwindled and dwindled steadily, until
> At last a scooped-out basin would not fill;
> And thenceforth 'twas a way of mocking dust (p. 168).

Still desire for revenge drives Hugh forward. He finds a little bread-root, eats enough to maintain consciousness, and then continues. Apart from this brief interlude describing Hugh's motivation and feeding, Neihardt continues with the same format of nature chronicling human progress:

> The coulee deepened; yellow walls flung high,
> Sheer to the ragged strip of blinding sky,
> Dazzled and sweltered in the glare of day.
> Capricious draughts that woke and died away
> Into the heavy drowse, were breatht as flame
> And midway down the afternoon ... (p. 169).

As Glass gains strength and makes progress in his crawl the use of landscape to describe his journey decreases proportionately. The references to landscape are generally preceded by "he saw" or followed by "he toiled" so that when Glass reaches the river we finally are told directly:

> Hugh set to work and built a little raft
> Of driftwood bound with grapevines. So it fell
> That one with an amazing tale to tell
> Came drifting to the gates of Kiowa (p. 221).

There is, no doubt, a form of redemption here, but there is also a prefiguring of Hugh's forgiveness of Jamie which concludes the *Song*.

Glass remains at the fort a while, so consumed with hatred and desire for revenge that he frightens those who observe him. One man, watching how Glass shakes with vengeance, remarks: "God fend that one should look with such a blizzard of a face for me" (p. 222). And here we see the wilderness of Glass's emotions from which he and Jamie must escape through the frank admission of guilt and its forgiveness.

Neihardt used this image of nature revealed in the human face to set the stage for his story-telling in *The Song of Jed Smith*, the last of the mountain men *Songs*. As that work begins two men are sitting at a campsite and a rider with a dog comes up the canyon bringing with him beef and a jug of Taos liquor. One of the men, Black Harris, recognizes the stranger as Bob Evans, a man who had in earlier years trapped with Jed Smith and others of the original Henry-Ashley crew. As they sit around the fire, talk moves to the death of Smith, killed by Comanches seven years before, and we are into the *Song of Jed Smith*. Neihardt's description of Bob Evans, his face reflected in the brightening light of the campfire, is worth noting:

> Leather-skinned,
> It was, hard-bitten by the worldly wind;
> But more the weather of a mind that seeks
> In solitude had etched upon the cheeks
> A cryptic story (p. 5).

Here nature and human character begin to become interchangeable qualities. Even more so we can see this synthesis in Black Harris's description of the day that a party of men, led by Jed Smith, saw the South Pass of the Rockies:

> From where we sat and looked, the prairie dropped
> Along the easy shoulder of a hill
> Into a left-hand valley. Things got still
> And kind of strange. The others, gathered round,
> Quit talking, and there wasn't any sound
> Except a bridle made it. Then it came —
> That funny sort of feeling, just the same
> I had out there a little while ago —
> A feel of somthing you could never know,
> But it was something big and still and dim

That wouldn't tell. *It seemed to come from him*
Just looking down the Sandy towards the Green (p. 17).

When we grant that discovering the South Pass was a historical
moment, it was only acclaimed as such in retrospect. Yet Neihardt
vests the importance of the moment in Smith's character, which is
the locus for the stillness and strange emotions that land creates in
the expedition.

The balance in *Jed Smith* between nature and men is achieved by
sometimes describing landscape in terms of ancient ruins, as when the
expedition first viewed Bryce Canyon, Utah:

> Where a high plateau
> Stretched southwardly, a million years or so
> Of rain had hewed a great unearthly town
> With colored walls and towers that looked down
> On winding streets not meant for men to tread.
> You half believed an angel race, long dead,
> Had built with airy, everlasting stuff
> They quarried from the sunrise in the rough
> And spent their lives in fashioning, and died
> Before the world got old (p. 29).

Angel men had created this masterpiece of nature, since its similarity
to works of humans was so great. Yet we have already seen in
Neihardt's speculations and reflections in *The River and I* his pro-
pensity to project familiar human artifactual structures onto natural
features. The Bad Lands, we discover in *The River and I*, were not bad
but a land of awe. Even more, they were

> Rows of huge colonial mansions with pillared porticos looked from their
> dizzy terraces across the stream to where soaring mosques and mystic
> domes of worship caught the sun. It was all like the visible dream of a
> master architect gone mad. Gaunt, sinister ruins of medieval castles
> sprawled down the slopes of unassailable summits. Grim brown towers,
> haughtily crenellated, scowled defiance on the unappearing foe. Titanic
> stools of stone dotted barren garden slopes, where surely gods had once
> strolled in that far time when the stars sang and the moon was young
> (pp. 141–42).

Whether mad architects or angel races of builders, Neihardt draws
his comparison between nature and human construction so tightly
that we see the interrelationship of things clearly.

In the synthesis which he achieves in *Jed Smith*, Neihardt allows human personality to reach beyond the machismo which he earlier posited with respect to the mountain men. Granted that they were tested, and tested themselves against the western lands. Nevertheless, in the end it is human compassion that Neihardt sees in the mountain men, not the superhuman qualities which he claimed to admire in *The River and I*. Coming back from California crossing the Great Salt Flats, Smith and three men nearly die. Bob Evans cannot go any further without water and Smith leaves him, finds water three miles away, and returns to save him. Evans remembers when it was dawn and they spotted something that appeared to be water:

> One look at 'Diah told
> The answer that I knew. It was an old
> Old man I saw a moment in his place,
> The look of something broken in his face
> That wasn't to be mended any more (p. 95).

And Evans says:

> For more than pity happened in that bleak,
> Forsaken moment when I saw him weak
> Upon that ridge. I'd just begun to love him,
> And something in the breaking manhood of him
> Was stronger than his old unbroken might (p. 96).

It seems strange that Neihardt would choose Jed Smith as his major character to conclude the mountain man segment of *A Cycle of the West*. While Smith was a unique character, perhaps the only Bible-toting mountain man of the period, nevertheless his exploits were hardly those of a prudent man. Over a period of three years Smith had made two California expeditions. Of the thirty-three men with him, twenty-six had been killed or died, and two of the remaining group deserted him. His trailblazing discoveries and difficulties with the land were a result of poor planning rather than courage or fearless questing after the unknown. He was killed by the Comanches on an ill-fated trip where he had not known the territory and had not made adequate preparations for the journey. But if Neihardt sought to exemplify the American spirit of innocent and haphazard confrontation with fate, he could not have picked a better specimen than Jed Smith.

Neihardt's use of landscape in *Jed Smith* is perhaps hampered by the structure of the story. Smith's journeys exemplified the first attempts to chart the unknown western deserts by the Americans, but, once choosing these trips to describe, one is left with a minimal number of events to describe, and must confront the task of describing what is essentially a homogenous and hostile nature. Neihardt's device of using two former acquaintances of Smith does introduce a different perception of the western adventure, but it falls considerably short of the drama of either *Three Friends* or *Hugh Glass* and seems to be something in the nature of an epitaph rather than a satisfactory conclusion to the saga of the mountain men.

When I read Neihardt's first three *Songs*, the sense of western lands leaps from the pages for me. His descriptions of the storms, coulees, buttes, and grasses ring true. The manner in which he deals with the loneliness which can often overtake a newcomer on the land shows that his early experiences on the Great Plains ingrained in him the native's love of the land. But his poetry also recalls a number of other writers who have attempted to use land or its presence to indicate something eternal and transcendent. I call to mind three writers: Margaret Mitchell, Ross Lockridge, and Robinson Jeffers. It may be unfair to compare two novelists and a stoical poet to Neihardt, who is an epic poet, but the presence of natural lands is so dominant in these three writers that I cannot help but draw the comparison.

In Margaret Mitchell's *Gone With The Wind* we have a chronicle of crinolines and cavaliers, a story of the Old South as romanticized as it can be, and a strong cast of characters. Although we are taken with the ruthlessness of Scarlett O'Hara and the swashbuckling nature of Rhett Butler, it is always the red earth of Tara that provides us with the fundamental framework of the novel. There is no doubt that the red clay of central Georgia has a very powerful attraction for its natives. Martin Luther King, in his famous speech at the reflecting pool in Washington, D.C., referred to the rich red clay as determinative of much of what America was. Yet Tara remains an inert, perhaps overconfident character in the novel, serene in the knowledge that eventually it will reign supreme.

Raintree County, a complex novel by Ross Lockridge, indeed his only work, is dominated by a brooding swamp within which lies the mysterious Raintree. Johnny Shawnessy spends his life looking for transcendent meaning to break in upon him and, like Earnest in the Great Stone Face, comes finally to realize that in living he has discovered the complicated meanings which attach themselves to human experiences. But the grounding of the novel in the Raintree only serves to anchor otherwise ordinary events in a cosmic framework which never responds directly or takes an active role in shaping the lives of the major characters. Like Tara, the land is a stationary center for activities that swirl around it.

Robinson Jeffers' pessimism, perhaps now seen as more realistic in the light of impending collapse of industrial civilization, revolves about two images: hawks and granite. His counsel for his readers is to seek freedom as the hawk and to preserve as does the granite. Man can never hope to overcome his frailties, but he must stoically trudge down the road upon which his feet have been set. Much of Jeffers' poetry approaches the stark and bitter landscape of *Jed Smith*, but where Neihardt finds compassion and humanity in weakness, Jeffers only hints at human qualities that would enable us to transcend our situation.

There are probably other writers and poets who deal more extensively with land, nature, and weather. I would suspect, however, that they do not materially transcend the use of these realities by Mitchell, Lockridge, and Jeffers to any great degree. In the three writers I have chosen for comparison I find an inert nature, a nature whose only role in the drama is to remain silent and confident until the puny human drama on its surface has finished and the characters are put away. With Neihardt, however, I see a vital and active landscape, a landscape I would characterize as having a "potential" and therefore in a sense being a "passive-active" character in the great western epics. Through his use of weather, Neihardt's particular specialty in *Three Friends*, through precise description, his forte in *Hugh Glass*, and through a balanced use of landscape and human strivings in *Jed Smith*, Neihardt gives us a landscape that at times can exert itself as a major force in the lives of human beings. Here we have a potential for relationship as a brooding presence, and we often realize that relationship. Land never simply sits there to be trod upon. It can and does become an integral part of the story, and without it we would not have the epic.

But land is never merely an obstacle over which humans march. Human problems and the relationship with land are always well-balanced and interwoven into a synthesis that tells a particular story.

It is important to note that this perception of land does not come as a result of Neihardt's involvement with Black Elk or the other Indians, Sioux and Omaha. In *The River and I* he describes his earliest involvement with the Missouri, so we are assured that his perception of the western lands is a native perception and not a doctrinal form of knowledge which he has derived from the Indians. In recognizing this fact we are brought even closer to the realization that lands can and do play an important role in human affairs. This truth was perceived best by the Indians who took some care to understand the land and who, after uncounted centuries of involvement with it, had revealed to them a complex set of ceremonies which enabled them to live harmoniously with the land. But Neihardt demonstrates that this intimacy with the land is not the exclusive property of a particular race of people. Rather it is the heritage of those whose roots go deep into the western soil.

In comparing Neihardt's use of land to contemporary literature which celebrates the outdoors — and there seems to be a plentitude of this literature — we can find only *The River and I* in which his attitudes approach the contemporary ecologist. We see this similarity in his speculations on how closely the Missouri breaks resemble human constructions of a by-gone civilization — castles and mosques. In *A Cycle of the West* we have a minimum use of descriptive phraseology celebrating either beauty of landscape or human romantic responses to it. Living in the out-of-doors is not a treat to the mountain men as it is to our modern backpackers. The beauty of the land in the *Songs* comes directly from Neihardt's accurate description of it; it is not presented as a human reflection of them.

There are certainly many other things which can be said of Neihardt's involvement with western lands, and no commentary can adequately cover the breadth of his perceptions. Nevertheless, it is important to begin to suggest tools of analysis by which we can probe more deeply into the manner in which he handled this important subject. In seeking to find the proper epic form to describe the western adventure, in attempting to become the Homer for this great band of seekers of the fleece, Neihardt had to recognize the distinction which the western lands allowed. Greek and Trojan mythology and epic poetry involved lands, and one cannot describe *The Odyssey* except in terms of many varied lands. But in every instance land is submerged under the human drama and never became a determinative force in the story. Neihardt knew that in telling the saga of the West his native landscape was the most important character, and as it made men respond to it the dramatic element of the story unfolded. We would do ourselves well to remember this elemental fact as we read *A Cycle of the West*. It tells us a great deal about ourselves.

Neihardt, Collier and the Continuity of Indian Life

Peter Iverson

IF A PERSON WERE ASKED to select the two people in this century who were most influential in shaping a new conception of the American Indian, one could not do much better than to name John Neihardt and John Collier — a poet and a Commissioner of Indian Affairs. These two men's impressions of the continuity of American Indian life, their manner of expressing their understanding, and their profoundly practical interpretation of the substance of Indian life continue to influence a new generation of Americans. Their words, now reduced to paper, will endure, like the Indians themselves, for many generations.

At first glance Neihardt and Collier might appear to have little in common. Neihardt was a Nebraskan, a poet; his life and works were shaped by the rural midwestern milieu. He wrote of the Plains tribes. Collier was a Georgian, a social crusader and reformer; his views were influenced primarily by his experiences in New York and by his years in New Mexico where he first encountered the Pueblo and Navajo Indians. Collier never really understood the Plains Indians. It was in the Plains, both northern and southern, that he met some of the most determined opposition to his policy of self-government and revived tribalism when he was Commissioner of Indian Affairs.

Peter Iverson teaches history at the University of Wyoming and has published several works on the history of Navajos and of other Indians.

No one could have predicted, given the basic facts of the lives of these two men, that they would have emerged from their life experiences with similar perspectives and comparable values and, above all, a shared appreciation of American Indian life and traditions. In the waning days of the Collier commissionership, when each man had completed the work for which he would become famous — John Neihardt for the writing of *Black Elk Speaks* and John Collier for the successful passage of the Indian Reorganization Act — their paths finally crossed. The Second World War had made it necessary for the government to exile the Bureau of Indian Affairs to Chicago because office space in the nation's capital was at a premium.

Neihardt had recently moved to Chicago from St. Louis where he had spent a large part of his adult life working for a newspaper and writing his poetry. He worked briefly for the YMCA in Chicago and then approached Collier, who immediately hired Neihardt as director of the Division of Information for the Bureau of Indian Affairs. For the next two years Neihardt edited the BIA monthly journal, *Indians at Work*, the popular house organ which emphasized the progressive programs and policies of the agency. Collier resigned as commissioner in 1945; after the war ended the Bureau moved back to Washington. Neihardt remained in the Midwest, his direct relationship with Collier ended.[1]

Collier and Neihardt still had many years to live. Although they had already accomplished much, they both had an important part of their work ahead of them. In his remaining twenty-two years, John Collier wrote many articles and volumes that enhanced his reputation as a thinker and activist and defended the record of his public life. His classic work, *Indians of the Americas*, was published in 1947; in the 1960's he completed *On the Gleaming Way* and his autobiography, *From Every Zenith*.[2] The first years after his commissionership had been marked by what Collier's friend and old associate,

[1] See Lucile F. Aly, *John G. Neihardt: A Critical Biography* (Amsterdam: Rodopi N. V., 1977) pp. 235–244, for a description of Neihardt's work in the Indian Service.

[2] Collier subtitled *Indians of the Americas* (New York: Mentor Books, 1947) "The Long Hope." *On The Gleaming Way* (Denver: Swallow Press, 1962) is subtitled: "Navajos, Eastern Pueblo, Zunis, Hopis, Apaches, and Their Land; and Their Meaning to the World."

D'Arcy McNickle, would term, "a return to negation."[3] But Collier joined in and led the good fight against the termination policy. Before his death he had the quiet satisfaction of realizing that termination as a national policy for Indians would not succeed.[4]

Neihardt, three years Collier's junior, outlived him by five years. Following his work in the Bureau of Indian Affairs, he completed *A Cycle of the West,* and *When The Tree Flowered,* a novelistic treatment of Oglala Sioux traditions, as well as two autobiographical works, *All is But a Beginning* and *Patterns and Coincidences.* He served as a poet-in-residence for two decades at the University of Missouri where he was a popular lecturer and intellectual companion. In the twilight of his life, when the interest in Indians was at its height, partially because of his book *Black Elk Speaks,* appearances on the Dick Cavett show helped to focus the national spotlight on his remarkable career. Neihardt, too, knew that such masterpieces as *Black Elk Speaks* would be read by countless people in the years to come.[5]

The two men shared more than long life, government service, and a deep interest in American Indians. What is most significant, I believe, about John Collier and John Neihardt is their certainty that American Indians would continue to survive as a people and that American Indians had something important to contribute to the rest of the world. Both men were drawn to certain mystic qualities inherent in Indian life and culture; they expressed their appreciation of this substance in rich and colorful language that communicated to a very large audience.[6]

Let us begin with a sketch of Collier, before turning our attention to Neihardt. Collier recalled in his autobiography that he had become

[3]D'Arcy McNickle, *Native American Tribalism: Indian Survivals and Renewals* (New York: Oxford University Press, 1973), pp. 103–12. McNickle calls the Collier years "a time of reassessment" which followed "years of attrition."

[4]See, for example, John Collier, "The American Indian," in Joseph B. Gittler, ed., *Understanding Minority Groups* (New York: John Wiley & Sons, Inc., 1956), pp. 33–51. Collier notes in this article that his view of Indian life is the same as many authorities. One of the authorities he cites is John Neihardt.

[5]In addition to Aly's biography, one may consult Blair Whitney, *John G. Neihardt* (Boston: G. K. Hall & Co., 1976) for biographical details.

[6]Aly notes briefly that "both believed in Indian autonomy and in the encouragement of Indian culture," but does not explore the matter additionally (p. 236).

fascinated with traditional rural life through camping trips in the Appalachian area when he was a young man. But his consuming interest in American Indians began when he was in his mid-thirties. He had been a social worker identified with progressive movements in New York for some time. Here he had come into contact with many European immigrant groups, and also come face to face with the ravages of industrialism and its concommitant isolation of the individual in urban America. Collier tried to encourage the survival of European ethnicity, which he saw as means of reducing individual isolation and despair. He sought to promote community where every institution was designed to reduce or eliminate it. His years in New York helped him identify many basic modern problems. Searching for answers and for relief from the ailments of the city, Collier traveled first to California and then, at the invitation of New York acquaintance Mabel Dodge Luhan, he came to Taos Pueblo in New Mexico.[7]

Collier arrived in northern New Mexico in December, 1920. He observed the seasonal ceremonies of the Pueblo Indians and he absorbed the striking ancient world which surrounded him at Taos. Here, in the shadows of the magnificent Wheeler Peak, Collier believed he had finally encountered what he had been seeking, a way of life and a sense of community that a distressed industrial world badly needed. The people and experience of Taos, Collier later wrote, "changed my life plan"; "Here was a reaching to the fire-fountain of life through a deliberate social action employing a complexity of many arts. Here was the psychical wonder-working we think we find in Greek drama . . . here it was a whole community which entered into the experience and knew it as a fact."[8]

And so John Collier began a deep and lasting involvement in the world of the American Indian. He spearheaded the movement which defeated the Bursum bill and other legislative measures which had

[7]This brief summary is drawn from several sources, including Kenneth R. Philp, *John Collier's Crusade for Indian Reform, 1920–1954* (Tucson: University of Arizona Press, 1977); Clayton R. Koppes, "From New Deal to Termination: Liberalism and Indian Policy, 1933–1953," *Pacific Historical Review*, XLVI (November 1977), pp. 543–566; Stephen J. Kunitz, "The Social Philosophy of John Collier," *Ethnohistory*, XVIII (1971), pp. 213-229; and Collier's own works.

[8]John Collier, *Indians of the Americas*, p. 10.

threatened Pueblo Indian rights. With others in the American Indian Defense Association which he founded, he promoted a review of then-existing Indian policy which resulted in a landmark study in 1928 — the Meriam Report — and he led the growing chorus questioning the Americanization policy of the late nineteenth and early twentieth centuries. With the advent of the Franklin D. Roosevelt Administration, the energetic reformer entered government and not only became Commissioner of Indian Affairs under the New Deal but held that post longer than any other person in American history. His years were an era unique for progressive accomplishments. His actions were easy to criticize in retrospect, but his tendency to impose solutions on long-standing problems was balanced by his ability to make the massive bureaucratic structures serve people. He altered fundamentally the manner in which both Indians and non-Indians perceived the Indian future. The Indians were not to be a vanishing race, he argued.[9]

Even today that perception stands out as a remarkable insight. In 1983 the myth of assimilation might still be persuasive; in 1920 it was assumed to be true without question or hesitation. How could it have been otherwise? American Indians had been passing through one of the bleakest periods of their long history. Their ancestral landholdings had been subjected to a persistent and continuous erosion. With the closing of the American frontier, announced by Professor Turner with great fanfare in the 1890's, and the cession of armed conflicts with the western tribes, pressures had redoubled to reduce American Indian land holdings. The General Allotment Act or

[9]For essentially critical perspectives, see Philp, *John Collier's Crusade*, and Lawrence C. Kelly, "John Collier and the Indian New Deal: An Assessment;" the latter is included in Jane F. Smith and Robert M. Kvasnicka, ed., *Indian-White Relations: A Persistent Paradox* (Washington, D.C.: Howard University Press, 1976), pp. 227–41. Kelly's paper, along with a companion effort by Philp, presented at a 1972 conference on the history of Indian-white relations held at the National Archives. D'Arcy McNickle upon that occasion presented a spirited rejoinder to the papers. His comments are also included in the Smith and Kvasnicka volume, pp. 251–57. McNickle, an Indian himself, remained sympathetic to Collier and what he had tried to achieve. I attended this conference, and later as a fellow at the Newberry Library's Center for the History of the American Indian, had good, long talks with McNickle about Collier and the Collier legacy. D'Arcy died in 1977; I thank him now for those talks and for the influence he has had upon my work.

Dawes Act of 1887 established the administrative structures and procedures to rapidly divest Indians of their ancestral landed heritage. By the 1920's Indians had lost nearly two-thirds of the land they had possessed only fifty years before. Moreover, this half-century had been marked by determined onslaughts against traditional tribal cultures and religious beliefs.

The general opinion of informed people was that Indians should become a part of America and should not be allowed to remain aloof from its culture, beliefs and institutions. American Indians, it held, should learn English, "the language of the most enterprising nationalities under the sun." They should become Christians. They should not practice the Sun Dance, the Snake Dance, or other pagan rituals which could not be easily understood by non-Indians. The goal of national Indian policy would be to make the Indians feel "at home" in America.[10]

In 1930, when John Neihardt set out with his son Sigurd for the Pine Ridge Reservation, John Collier was not yet Indian commissioner. The gloom and despair which had begun with the Wounded Knee massacre still lingered in the minds of the old men and women at Pine Ridge and elsewhere. They looked back to the nineteenth century when they were young, free, and secure in their traditions. They remembered the steadily increasing pressures the white men brought to their land and lives. They recalled the triumphs on the Bozeman Trail and at the Little Big Horn, but they also recalled quite vividly what Black Elk would later label "the butchering at Wounded Knee":

> It was a good winter day when all this happened. The sun was shining. But after the soldiers marched away from their dirty work, a heavy snow began to fall. The wind came up in the night. There was a big blizzard, and it grew very cold. The snow drifted deep in the crooked gulch, and it was one long grave of butchered women and children and babies, who had never done any harm and were only trying to run away.[11]

Even the passage of time could not erase these images. Neihardt

[10]See the introduction to Francis Paul Prucha, ed., *Americanizing the American Indian: Writings by the "Friends of the Indian," 1880–1900* (Cambridge: Harvard University Press, 1973).

[11]*Black Elk Speaks* (Lincoln: University of Nebraska Press, 1961), p. 268.

returned to the reservation the next year with his daughters and in
conversation with Black Elk and some other Oglala elders began to
transcribe the information that would fill the classic book on the
Sioux. There were times, he once confessed, when the barrier of language disappeared and the two minds, Black Elk's and Neihardt's,
worked as one in transmitting the reality of traditional Sioux life.

The final chapter of *Black Elk Speaks* is entitled" "The End of the
Dream." The narration of the book follows the course of Black Elk's
life and concludes in this chapter with Black Elk looking back "from
this high hill of my old age." In his mind he sees the dead at Wounded
Knee as clearly as during the incident and he reflects, "and I can see
that something else died there in the bloody mud, and was buried in
the blizzard. A people's dream died there. It was a beautiful dream."
The last two sentences of the book are perhaps the best remembered
and most often quoted of all of Neihardt's writing: "And I, to whom
so great a vision was given in my youth — you see me now a pitiful
old man who has done nothing, for the nation's hoop is broken and
scattered. There is no center any longer, and the sacred tree is dead"
(p. 276).

It seems to me that it is singularly unfortunate that those two
sentences ring the loudest in the public memory. This is not to mini-
mize the horror of Wounded Knee nor to deny that it may be viewed
as the end of an age. But it was not the end of the Sioux, let alone
the termination of American Indian life. In altered and increasingly
adaptive forms, Indian existence continued and the people endured
their hardships. Indeed, even in this very region, the Sioux people
would soon begin to undertake important transitional steps from that
cherished past into the uncertain future under the provisions of the
Indian Reorganization Act that would make their reservations less
like prisons and more akin to the cultural homelands they wished
to preserve.[12]

John Neihardt, I think, understood that this transition was taking
place. He valued the old ways and honored them both in *Black Elk
Speaks* and in *When the The Tree Flowered*, capturing as no man

[12]See, for example, Frederick Hoxie, "From Prison to Homeland: The Cheyenne River Indian Reservation before WW I," *South Dakota History*, X, 1 (Winter 1979), pp. 1–24.

before or since the flavor of the Sioux idiom. Black Elk's story is told through John Neihardt, but so skillful is Neihardt's writing that few readers remember that it is Neihardt recounting what he has been told. Neihardt was more than a translator or recording secretary. When one reads passages from other Neihardt works, his role is more clear. The imagery and language of *When the Tree Flowered* and *A Cycle of the West* echo *Black Elk Speaks*; the message and substance of the volume belong to Black Elk but the mode of expression is most certainly Neihardt's. As Neihardt said in 1971 when asked about the relationship of the two men in writing the book:

> *Black Elk Speaks* is a work of art with two collaborators, the chief one being Black Elk. My function was both creative and editorial. I think he knew the kind of person I was when I came to see him — I am referring to the mystical strain in me and all my work . . . At times considerable editing was necessary, but it was always worth the editing. The beginning and ending are mine; they are what he would have said if he had been able. At times I changed a word, a sentence, sometimes created a paragraph. And the translation — or rather the transformation — of what was given me was expressed so that it could be understood by the white world.[13]

Neihardt felt that Black Elk had an important message and that the message should be heard beyond his circle of acquaintances. In the preface to *Black Elk Speaks*, Neihardt says that Black Elk related his story "in fulfillment of a duty that he felt incumbent upon him. His chief purpose was to 'save his Great Vision for men.'" Neihardt's accomplishment, then, was to save that vision and to share it permanently with the rest of the world against the time when people might have a better understanding of it.[14]

Often forgotten in the attention paid to the conclusion of *Black Elk Speaks*, is the postscript which Neihardt appended to the narration. This postscript is much more than an epilogue or an afterthought. Neihardt must have included the four pages because he did not want the book to end negatively, so he describes Black Elk gazing across the desolate Badlands of South Dakota, at Harney Peak, the ancient center of the Sioux universe. Black Elk recalls being taken in his

[13]Sally McCluskey, "*Black Elk Speaks* and So Does John Neihardt," *Western American Literature*, VI (Winter 1972), p. 238.

[14]*Black Elk Speaks*, p. xi.

youthful vision to the center of the earth and being shown "all the good things in the sacred hoop of the world." Black Elk wishes to go to Harney Peak "to say something to the Six Grandfathers before he dies" (p. 277).

Therefore Neihardt and Black Elk travel to the Black Hills, to Harney Peak, and there Black Elk cries out, sending "a voice for a people in despair." He asserts that the sacred tree has not bloomed as he had seen it in his earlier vision. But all is not lost: "It may be that some little root of the sacred tree still lives. Nourish it then, that it may leaf and bloom and fill with singing birds. Hear me, not for myself, but for my people; I am old. Hear me that they may once more go back into the sacred hoop and find the good red road, the shielding tree!" A slight drizzle tenderly falls on the old man standing at the center of his world. The old man weeps silently. Neihardt's final sentence tells us that "In a little while the sky was clear again" (pp. 277–80).

Black Elk Speaks appeared in 1932; John Collier became Commissioner of Indian Affairs in April of the following year and within a year of taking office had secured passage of the Indian Reorganization Act giving self-government back to the Indians. American Indians were on the long and tedious trail back. Both Neihardt and Collier remain important for their testimony to the special quality of the Indian spirit at a time when most Americans still assumed that Indians would eventually disappear. More than that, they each helped the Indians recapture the strength and opportunity to regenerate themselves.

Collier once wrote that Indians "disclose that social heritage is far more perduring than is commonly believed." "On how small a life base," he observed in language strikingly similar to that of Neihardt, "on a diminished and starved land-base for how many generations, the motivations and expectations of a society, and its world-view and value system and loyalties, can keep themselves alive; how these social possessions, which are of the soul, can endure, like the roots and seeds on the Mojave desert, through long ages, without one social rain; and how they rush, like these roots and seeds, into surprising and wonderful blossom when the social rain does come at last." John Neihardt surely agreed with John Collier that the Indian experience told us that the "sunken stream can flow again, the ravaged desert can bloom, the great past is not killed."[15] It is singularly important that, when visualizing social and communal growth and regeneration, Collier, Neihardt and Black Elk all choose the root as the symbol of enduring values.

John Neihardt called the first part of his autobiography, the last volume published before his death, *All is But a Beginning*. In it, he added another postscript. He wondered aloud about the next generation and the world in which he had grown old. In spite of the unhappy signs and events he witnessed in the America of the early 1970's, he sensed a resurgence of interest in the things of the spirit, a "spiritual longing." He concluded *All is But a Beginning* with "a slogan that I wish to leave with my young friends to be recalled for courage, like a battle cry, in times of great stress." It derived from a Sioux friend who as a youth had undertaken a vision quest. He had fasted and prayed, but no vision had come. He despaired. But finally, "a great cry came from overhead like a fearless warrior hailing his wavering comrade in the heat of battle. 'Hoka-hey, brother — Hold fast, hold fast, there is more!' Looking up, he saw an eagle soaring yonder on a spread of mighty wings — and it was the eagle's voice he heard." Neihardt recalls the old man, intently listening, and feeling a power run through him that never left.[16]

"There is more!" might be understood as the creed which John Collier and John Neihardt adopted. Whether prominent or hidden in obscurity neither man ever doubted the validity of his central vision. In each, concern for the human spirit shown brightly, and both found within the American Indian tradition a sense of relatedness which they felt should be shared with the world. In their outspoken advocacy of things Indian they provided the necessary leadership to assist Indian people in re-establishing themselves. Thus two unlikely individuals from another culture championed the aspirations and values at the root of Indian life. The fearless recognition of Indians by John Collier and John Neihardt made them two of the most influential individuals in Indian affairs in our time.

[15]Collier, *Indians of the Americas*, p. 171.

[16]*All is But a Beginning: Youth Remembered, 1881-1901* (New York: Harcourt Brace Jovanovich, Inc., 1972) pp. 170-173.

John G. Neihardt's Lakota Legacy

Raymond J. DeMallie

NO AUTHOR, EITHER WHITE OR INDIAN, has yet written about the Lakota people in terms that bring their traditional religion and culture to life more convincingly than John G. Neihardt. He wrote of the Lakotas so that they seem like real people to readers of all races and their suffering is magnified into the suffering of humanity. His works are true literature, transcending the particular without destroying it, interpreting Lakota culture and creating a place for Lakota religion in the ranks of nonwestern philosophies to which we western people continually look for inspiration.

To the Lakota people of today, Neihardt's writings, especially his personal interpretation of the teachings of the Oglala holy man Black Elk, strike resonant chords that have elevated *Black Elk Speaks*, as Vine Deloria, Jr., suggests, to the status of an American Indian Bible.[1] Perhaps the comparison is not apt; the book might better be considered an American Indian Rosetta Stone, for it serves both Indians and non-Indians of today as a way into the traditional native American

Raymond J. DeMallie, associate professor of anthropology at Indiana University, is the editor of *The Sixth Grandfather: Black Elk's Teachings Given to John G. Neihardt.* He wishes to acknowledge gratefully Hilda Neihardt Petri's willingness to discuss her experiences with her father on the Pine Ridge Reservation in 1931 and 1944; her personal perspective has been crucial to the understanding of Neihardt presented here. Special acknowledgement must also be made to the kindness with which Dr. Lucile F. Aly gave the first draft of this paper a critical reading; her efforts much improved both the content and style.

[1]Vine Deloria, Jr., "Introduction," *Black Elk Speaks* (Lincoln: University of Nebraska Press, 1979), p. xiii.

culture of the nineteenth century, a key to translation from modern English into older American Indian modes of thought. Ella C. Deloria, the native Sioux linguist, wrote to Neihardt on March 18, 1932:

> I have just finished *Black Elk Speaks.* I want you to know that it makes me happy and sad all at once — sad for the days that are gone, and glad that a white man really lives who can enter into a right understanding of a Dakota's vision, and can translate it into so poetic a form.[2]

What was Neihardt's genius that so fitted him to the role of interpreter for the Lakotas? What were his experiences with the Lakota people that provided him the understanding that, judging from their writings, dozens of anthropologists, journalists, and historians seemed to have missed? The answers are complex but all revolve around the intensity of the interaction betwen Neihardt and Black Elk; through this one teacher Neihardt developed his understanding of the Lakotas.

Neihardt's legacy of writings on the Lakotas, based on his interviews with Black Elk, comprises three works. The first is *Black Elk Speaks* (1932), the most famous and most frequently read of Neihardt's books. As the biography of a Lakota Holy Man, it is also undoubtedly the most misunderstood of Neihardt's Lakota works. Subsequent to its publication, the author has been faced with a double charge: on the one hand, that the work represented Neihardt's own philosophy expressed under the guise of an Indian autobiography; on the other hand, that the work was merely a direct transcription of the words of Black Elk, for which Neihardt should not pretend to claim an author's credit. Both accusations saddened him, for the critics missed the real dynamic of the book, the electric energy of the meeting of two like minds from two different cultures.

The book is Black Elk's story, but the structure and form — and more importantly, the tone — are Neihardt's. As he said in an interview:

> *Black Elk Speaks* is a work of art with two collaborators, the chief one being Black Elk. My function was both creative and editorial. . . . The beginning and the ending [of the book] are mine; they are what he would have said if he had been able. . . . And the translation — or rather the

[2]Neihardt Collection, Western Historical Manuscripts Collection, University of Missouri — Columbia.

transformation — of what was given me was expressed so that it could be understood by the white world.[3]

After its initial publication, Neihardt considered *Black Elk Speaks* to be a literary failure. Although reviewers were generally favorable, the book failed to capture the popular market and was in time remaindered. Only upon its republication in 1960 did it find a place with the counter-culture movements of that decade and catapult to fame. In the end the book has fulfilled Black Elk's trust, a sacred duty placed on Neihardt, that together they could make the sacred tree bloom for their children.[4]

The second work of the legacy is *The Song of the Messiah* (1935), the fifth and last volume of Neihardt's epic poem, *A Cycle of the West*. The work tells in verse the story of the Lakotas' acceptance of the Ghost Dance in 1889 and of the senseless misunderstanding between Indians and non-Indians that exploded in the Wounded Knee massacre of 1890. Black Elk's own story is interwoven in the narrative, whose theme, as Neihardt expressed it, is "the triumph of spirit through apparent defeat."[5] The defeat of the Lakotas at Wounded Knee is a sad ending to the innocent lives of those who died there; but the spirit lives and triumphs to tell a cautionary tale for future generations — the message is the unity of the human spirit and the common purpose of all individuals' lives. Of the three works, this is the strongest expression of Neihardt's own interpretation of the Lakotas as representatives of the human condition. Unfortunately, the poetic form seems archaic to readers today and now it is also the least read of the three.

The third book, *When The Tree Flowered* (1951; British edition entitled *Eagle Voice*, 1953), was born of Neihardt's frustration that *Black Elk Speaks* had failed to tell the Lakotas' story to the world. In this work he used the life story of Eagle Elk, an aged Oglala warrior, to provide the narrative structure. (The man's name was Eagle Elk,

[3]Sally McCluskey, *"Black Elk Speak* and So Does John Neihardt," *Western American Literature*, VI (Winter 1972), pp. 238–39.

[4]See Lucile F. Aly, *John G. Neihardt: A Critical Biography* (Amsterdam: Rodopi, N.V., 1977), p. 174. Throughout, I have relied on Dr. Aly's superb work both for biographical and critical details.

[5]Aly, p. 177.

but to avoid confusion with Black Elk, Neihardt decided to call him Eagle Voice in the book.) Although he termed it a novel, the book is as faithful to the interview material as *Black Elk Speaks*. The bulk of the material in *When The Tree Flowered* is taken from interviews with Black Elk that focused on Lakota history and the details of Lakota social order and culture. This material is a true native history, replete with tales and anecdotes that serve as exegesis to the fundamental structure. The book masterfully combines Black Elk's tales and history with the universal human story of Eagle Elk's life and loves to form a work that captures the essence of the traditional Lakota way of life more fully and dramatically than either of the earlier works. Neihardt's categorization of it as fiction suggests far more artifice and invention than actually characterizes the work.

Each of these three books replicates the other in basic coverage and message. Thematically, each tries in a different way to represent the struggle between the Lakotas and the whites as a part of the overall history of humanity. The fundamental difference of Lakota culture from that of the whites, the inevitable clash between the two cultures, and the final horror of Wounded Knee as a symbolic end to the old Lakota culture, form the dramatic themes.

A real understanding of Neihardt's books depends upon a full knowledge of his method of gathering material and his means of rendering it in literary form. Long before Neihardt met Black Elk, he was well acquainted with Indians, both Omahas and Sioux. He had already published two volumes of short stories concerning Indian and frontier life based on his experiences in Nebraska — *The Lonesome Trail* (1907) and *Indian Tales and Others* (1926) — as well as *The Song of the Indian Wars* (1925), the fourth volume of his epic, covering the Sioux and Cheyenne struggle with the U.S. Army from the mid-1860s until the death of Cràzy Horse in 1877. In 1925 he had begun writing *The Song of the Messiah*, the last volume of the *Cycle*; it took ten years to complete. Although the facts of the Ghost Dance and the ensuing struggle with the army became clear enough, Neihardt felt that he lacked an understanding of the emotional qualities — "the deeper spiritual significance" — of the Ghost Dance. In August 1930 Neihardt visited Pine Ridge with his son Sigurd, searching, as he later wrote, for some old medicine man who had been deeply involved in the Ghost Dance. "What I needed for my purposes was something to be experienced through intimate contact, rather than something to be received through telling." It was then that he met Black Elk, at his home near Manderson on the Pine Ridge Reservation.[6]

That first meeting was momentous. During four and one-half hours of talk, the two men struck a remarkable rapport. Black Elk decided immediately to entrust his great vision to Neihardt. He said, "As I sit here, I can feel in this man beside me a strong desire to know the things of the Other World. He has been sent to learn what I know, and I will teach him." Neihardt, for his part, was excited to learn about the old Lakota religion, even though it was the Ghost Dance he had come to learn about. On August 10, 1930, he wrote to his friend, Julius T. House, of the strong rapport he felt with the old medicine man: "Very often it seemed as though I, myself, were telling the things he told me, but I got something from him that I cannot describe." Black Elk gave Neihardt a pendant representing the morning star, a Lakota symbol of wisdom, and told him to return in the spring when he would teach him the sacred things. Soon after Neihardt returned home to Branson, Missouri, he wrote to Black Elk, "I do feel that so much is known by you Indians that our white people do not know and should know, that I am very eager to write this book if you will help me."[7]

In October 1930, William Morrow and Co. offered Neihardt a contract for a book about Black Elk and provided a small advance to finance the work. Accompanied by his daughters Enid and Hilda, Neihardt returned to Pine Ridge on May 9, 1931. They found Black Elk ready and eager. Enid wrote:

> We drove into Manderson and met Black Elk's youngest son and his older son. They were down there getting beds for us. When we got to the Black Elks' place, following the boys, we found that he had made many arrangements for us and apparently he considered this as one of the great things of his life.[8]

[6]Preface, *Black Elk Speaks*, p. xv.
[7]Preface, p. xvii; shorthand drafts of letters to House and Black Elk, Neihardt Collection.
[8]Diary of Enid Neihardt, Neihardt Collection.

The local trader had provided material for a large tepee on which Black Elk painted the symbols of his vision; this served both as a forum and as lodging for the Neihardts during their stay. Newly-cut pines had been brought in to form a sunshade and as a special accommodation for the white visitors, a starkly new privy had been erected conveniently close to the house.[9]

The next morning Black Elk began to speak of his vision experiences. A number of other old men were invited, including Standing Bear, Fire Thunder, Chase In The Morning, and Holy Black Tail Deer. Their presence validated Black Elk's statements and symbolized the gravity and importance of the occasion. The event was public; other old men would ride up and sit on the ground, their backs to the proceedings, until they were invited to join. The extra mouths proved an economic burden and Enid worried in her journal that they might soon have to feed the whole Sioux nation!

The interviews from which *Black Elk Speaks* was written occupied sixteen days: May 10 and May 14-28. On the 29th the Neihardts and Black Elk and his son Ben drove to the Black Hills. On May 30th the party climbed Harney Peak for Black Elk's prayer to the Six Grandfathers. Later that day they separated, the Black Elks driving back to Manderson in Ben's Ford, and the Neihardts beginning their trip home to Missouri.

The brevity of these interviews makes the accomplishment of *Black Elk Speaks* seem all the greater. Both men dedicated their all to the work, and although it seemed to the Neihardt daughters that it progressed excruciatingly slowly as the process of translation shuffled back and forth between the two languages, the amount of material they recorded is impressive. Enid wrote, on May 23:

> This morning, Saturday morning, we had another day of work out under the pine shelter here at Black Elk's place. We got a few good things today, but not nearly so many as we got the day before. The main thing was history today and Black Elk is not nearly so good at remembering his history as he is in telling things about himself. When he talks about his vision he is marvelous!

[9]Preface; Aly, *John G. Neihardt*, pp. 170-71; interviews with Hilda Neihardt Petri, Columbia, Missouri.

Enid served as secretary, taking down the interviews in shorthand. These stenographic notes, of course, are several degrees removed from Black Elk's actual narrative. As Black Elk told his story, his son Ben translated into English, sentence by sentence. When necessary, questions were put to the old man to clarify the meaning. Neihardt restated each sentence orally, standardizing some of Ben's rather idiomatic "Indian English," and the final sentence was written down by Enid Neihardt, as she heard it. During the earlier portion of the interviews, the story of Black Elk's visions, the stenographic notes are somewhat more sketchy and less grammatical; they soon become much more grammatical and full as the system of translation and transcription improved. After returning to Branson, Enid made a typescript of her notes, rearranging them in the chronological order of Black Elk's life and amplifying the grammar and clarifying meaning when necessary to make a smooth narrative. It was from this typescript that Neihardt wrote *Black Elk Speaks* and while it is as close as possible to the old man's words, it must be understood that the process of translation and recording make it different from a verbatim record.[10]

As the interviews progressed, the inexplicable rapport between Neihardt and Black Elk deepened so that each seemed to anticipate what the other would say next. It almost seemed that they were sharing the same body of knowledge about the other world of the spirit. Neihardt wrote to House on June 3, 1931:

> A strange thing happened often while I was talking with Black Elk. Over and over he seemed to be quoting from my poems, and sometimes I quoted some of my stuff to him which when translated into Sioux could not retain much of its literary character, but the old man immediately recognized the ideas as his own. There was an uncanny merging of consciousness between the old fellow and myself. . . .[11]

After Neihardt had heard Black Elk's vision, he told the old man about a dream he himself had had when eleven years old that in some ways paralleled Black Elk's experience. Like Black Elk, Neihardt had

[10]For a discussion of the significance of translation see Kenneth Lincoln, "Word Senders," *American Indian Culture and Research Journal*, IV, 1–2 (1980), pp. 2–4.

[11]Neihardt Collection.

fallen suddenly ill. In the dream he saw himself flying through space, arms and hands forward, much as Black Elk had followed the two messengers to the rainbow tepee. In Neihardt's dream, as he described it, there was empty vastness and dreadful speed, a great Voice driving him on. The dream recurred three times during the night; in the morning the fever was gone and he was well. Neihardt interpreted the dream as a pattern for his life, driving him to strive for success in his literary work, a spiritual striving for a higher conception of human existence. Nearly twenty years later, Neihardt wrote a poem entitled "The Ghostly Brother," identifying the cosmic force of the dream with a spiritual alter ego, a fate, a guide: "I am you and you are I." The poem expresses tension betwen the two egos, the spiritual leading forward, urging the other to follow "Through the outer walls of sense," and towards a higher reality, while the earthly ego fears the challenge and begs to stop and enjoy life's wordly comforts. The poem is an important expression of Neihardt's personal quest for meaning in life.[12]

Neihardt also related to Black Elk some of the wonderful coincidences of his life, things he was at a loss to explain. Most dramatic was the experience in the writing of *The Song of Hugh Glass* (1915), which required him to describe in detail the spot on the Grand River where Glass was mauled by a bear and to describe the details of the terrain as Glass crawled downriver to Fort Kiowa. Since Neihardt had never visited the area, he had to imagine the landscape. In 1923 he had the opportunity to accompany a group of friends who had decided to erect a monument to Glass at the site of his mishap. Much to Neihardt's surprise, the old bank of the Grand (its course having subsequently shifted) was exactly as he had described it in the poem.[13]

When he heard this story, Black Elk found no surprise in it. He said to Neihardt,

> This was a power vision that you had. The dream when you were eleven years old. It was your brother ghost who had the power to describe that land that you did not see and had been helping you to do all these other

[12]For the dream see *All Is But A Beginning: Youth Remembered, 1881–1901* (New York: Harcourt Brace Jovanovich, Inc., 1972), pp. 47–49. The poem appears in *The Quest* (New York: The Macmillan Company, 1928), pp. 175–78.
[13]Aly, *John G. Neihardt*, pp. 83–84.

things. I think this was an Indian brother from the happy hunting grounds who is your guide.

Black Elk was convinced that Neihardt had been sent to him as part of a cosmic plan to save his vision for the world. He told Neihardt:

> Before I ever saw you I wondered about the dream and your brother ghost has put you here to do good to your people and through you your people have their knowledge. Furthermore, this vision of mine ought to go out, I feel, but somehow I couldn't get anyone to do it. I would think about it and get sad. I wanted the world to know about it. It seems that your ghostly brother has sent you here to do this for me. You are here and have the vision just the way I wanted and then the tree will bloom again and the people will know the true facts. We want this tree to bloom in the world of truth that doesn't judge.

For Black Elk, this was another chance to fulfill his sacred duty given to him in the vision. He had failed in the past, as he admitted to Neihardt:

> I should have done my deed and because I did not do it I have been punished. I should have gone through my vision and performed everything on earth and then I would have prospered. At the same time the tree that was to bloom just faded away but the roots will stay alive and we are here to make that tree bloom.

Neihardt became for Black Elk a living part of his great vision, its means of fulfillment. This is why he gave him the name Flaming Rainbow. Not only was the flaming rainbow a central feature of his great vision, marking the entrance to the cloud tepee of the Six Grandfathers, but it was also the subject of the last vision that Black Elk told Neihardt about, one which he had during the ghost dances. In this last vision he had seen the flaming rainbow and the cloud tepee once again, while overhead an eagle soared and called out to him, "Remember this." Now that vision must have seemed to Black Elk to have been a prophecy.

In giving Neihardt the name Flaming Rainbow, Black Elk said to him,

> You are a word sender. The earth is like a garden and over it your words go like rain making it green and after your words have passed the memory of them will stand long in the West like a Flaming Rainbow.[14]

[14]Shorthand draft, Neihardt to House, June 3, 1931; Neihardt Collection.

The colors of the rainbow itself were symbols of Neihardt's words and thoughts and the power they would have to express the truth and goodness of the vision. Neihardt accepted the name with pride and bore it in the spirit in which it was given, as token of his sacred duty to Black Elk to make the vision and the Lakota people known to the world.

For Black Elk, relating his vision to Neihardt was not merely a sharing, but an actual transfer. In giving him the name, Black Elk adopted Neihardt as a son and passed down to him the power and responsibilities of the vision. As he related the vision to Neihardt he told him, in the words of Enid's transcript, that he had "a queer feeling all the time he is telling this, and that he is giving his power away. He feels that he will die very soon afterward." To his publisher, William Morrow, Neihardt wrote that Black Elk seemed melancholy at the thought of having at last given away his great vision:

> Once he said to me, "Now I have given you my vision that I have never given to anyone before and with it I have given you my power. I have no power now, but you can take it and perhaps with it you can make the tree bloom again, at least for my people and for yourself."[15]

Back home in Branson, Neihardt was excited about the writing of Black Elk's story, to be called "The Tree That Never Bloomed." He wrote to Morrow asking about the possibilities of promoting a motion picture version of Black Elk's horse dance. "Black Elk has said that he would produce this dance for me with a whole village as a background if I could interest the movie people." Morrow thought that a dramatization of Black Elk's life would make a better subject and Neihardt's dreams for a major movie loomed large; although he tried for years to interest producers, the project failed to materialize. It would have provided Black Elk the opportunity to enact his vision on earth and to share it most fully with the world.

In June, 1931, Neihardt wrote to reassure Black Elk:

> Enid is now copying on the typewriter the notes she took of your story, and very soon I shall be able to get to work on the book. It is going to be a really big book, and you are going to be happy about it I know. Keep this in mind when you feel lonesome or sad and it will cheer you up. The

[15]Shorthand draft, Neihardt to Morrow, June, 1931; Neihardt Collection.

finest things in your life are going to be saved for other men. This ought to make you happy.[16]

Neihardt wrote the book at an inspired rate; by October it was complete. The publisher, more interested in an Indian adventure story than a philosophical treatise, objected to the long chapter on the great vision and suggested relegating it to an appendix. Neihardt stood firm, but he relented on the title, which the publisher thought did not adequately represent the subject of the book. The title *Black Elk Speaks* was a compromise, suggested by Neihardt's wife Mona.

Neihardt was an extraordinarily faithful spokesman for Black Elk. Although his psychic empathy for Black Elk might have led him to take great liberties with the material, he did not do so. Comparison of *Black Elk Speaks* to Enid's stenographic record of the interviews only underscores the fidelity of Neihardt's literary interpretation.[17] In *Black Elk Speaks*, Neihardt retained the intensely personal quality of the interviews. Traditional Lakota culture is presented through Black Elk's own life experiences. The old Lakota religion is embodied in Black Elk's childhood vision in which he was taken to meet the Six Grandfathers, the Powers of the Universe, and was shown the path that his people would follow through four generations. He was shown the troubled times that lay ahead, but he was given specific herbs and powers to help his people.

Throughout the book, the history of the Lakotas' struggle with the whites is presented as a backdrop for Black Elk's personal quest to find the way to implement his power. In vain he searches for some way to use his vision to restore his people to the sacred hoop and to make the tree flower, the symbol of well being and of the continuity of the Lakotas as a people. Following Lakota custom, Black Elk enacted some parts of his vision as sacred ceremonies and thus gained mastery over the powers given him, enabling him to cure individuals suffering illness. But as the Lakotas settled at their agencies, and the buffalo herds disappeared, there seemed no way to implement the great vision as a whole and thereby save the people. Neihardt wrote

[16]Letter in the Neihardt Collection.

[17]The stenographic record of Neihardt's interviews with Black Elk, edited by the present author, is published as *The Sixth Grandfather: Black Elk's Teachings Given To John G. Neihardt* (Lincoln: University of Nebraska Press, 1984).

in *Black Elk Speaks,* voicing Black Elk's feelings: "The nation's hoop was broken, and there was no center any longer for the flowering tree. The people were in despair."[18]

At age twenty-two, in 1886, Black Elk decided to join Buffalo Bill's Wild West Show as a way of seeing the white man's world. Speaking again for Black Elk, Neihardt wrote, "Maybe if I could see the great world of the Wasichu, I could understand how to bring the sacred hoop together and make the tree to bloom again at the center of it." This experiment was not a success. "All the time I was away from home across the big water, my power was gone, and I was like a dead man moving around most of the time" (pp. 218–19, 235).

When he returned to Pine Ridge in 1889, Black Elk heard about the Ghost Dance prophet Wovoka. He thought perhaps the two of them had had the same vision and that together they could save the people and restore the sacred hoop. When he saw a ghost dance for the first time, Black Elk was astonished that it so closely resembled his great vision, the people dancing in a circle around a central tree. "This was to remind me to get to work at once and help to bring my people back into the sacred hoop. . . . I believed my vision was becoming true at last, and happiness overcame me" (p. 242).

The Ghost Dance was to prove a false hope. While he danced, Black Elk had a vision of the flaming rainbow from his great vision, and later he interpreted this as a sign that he had been misled in placing his faith in the Ghost Dance. The Wounded Knee massacre was the final blow. "When I saw this," Black Elk said, "I wished that I had died too." In the last paragraphs of the main text of *Black Elk Speaks,* Neihardt sums up this feeling of despair:

> I did not know then how much was ended. When I look back now from this high hill of my old age, I can still see the butchered women and children lying heaped and scattered all along the crooked gulch as plain as when I saw them with eyes still young. And I can see that something else died there in the bloody mud, and was buried in the blizzard. A people's dream died there. It was a beautiful dream.
>
> And I, to whom so great a vision was given in my youth — you see me now a pitiful old man who has done nothing, for the nation's hoop is

[18]*Black Elk Speaks* (New York: William Morrow & Company, 1932), p. 218. All quotations are cited to the pagination of the first edition.

broken and scattered. There is no center any longer, and the sacred tree is dead (pp. 266, 276).

The author's postscript relates Black Elk's prayer on Harney Peak. There, before Neihardt and his daughters, the old man prayed that the sacred tree might bloom again and the people find their way back to the sacred hoop and the good red road. "O make my people live!" In reply a low rumble of thunder sounded, and a drizzle of rain fell out of a sky that shortly before had been cloudless. Whether the sign was a hopeful one, or only a tragic recognition of the power that Black Elk had been given but failed to use is one of the dynamic issues that makes the book a literary success. In his letter to William Morrow, Neihardt reported that after the prayer, Black Elk "seemed broken and very sad." But in the book Neihardt records only the facts as they happened, calling them "merely a more or less striking coincidence," and allowing the reader to interpret the event as he will. But to Neihardt, as to Black Elk, nothing was ever mere coincidence (pp. 277–80).[19]

Black Elk Speaks may be best characterized as an elegy. It recognizes the tragedy of a man who tried but failed in his life's mission; at the same time it commemorates a way of life that has passed and a people who must also pass. Neihardt's admiration for the old-time Indians was immense, but their descendants, he felt, had to mingle with the rest of American society in order to survive. When he returned from his visit with Black Elk, Neihardt wrote a letter to the Secretary of the Interior by way of report that eloquently expresses his feeling at that time:

> As you, of course, already know, the Ogalalas are hardly a happy or a prosperous people and those who fancy that they could be made so through political reforms and by measly "practical" measures, do not understand the Indian consciousness. I did not go there in a criticizing spirit nor did I come away in any such mood. While I was among the old men and feeling deeply the profound spirituality of which they are capable, funny as this may seem to one who does not know Indians well,

[19]Shorthand draft of letter to Morrow, June, 1931; Neihardt Collection. For Neihardt's feelings about coincidence see his *Patterns and Coincidences: A Sequel To All Is But A Beginning* (Columbia: University of Missouri Press, 1978), pp. 1–2.

I had a dream of what might be done for these Ogalalas if the effort could be made. The simple fact about them is that they cannot be turned into white men and as a people they cannot be supervised successfully after our fashion. They are visionary, lively, and improvident for very good reasons. One feels that they as a people have lost their self-respect and that the only way they could be made really happy and prosperous would be through some revival of their own courageousness and their own religion. Incidentally, they had the courageousness and the spirit both and in the course of this study they are indeed seen to be admirable. There were times when I felt very humble before those old men especially when Black Elk, who is in spirit a great poet, was describing the great vision upon which his whole life has been based. What a pity it seems that these people, who are living now in what amounts to a social vacuum, could not be encouraged to revive and cherish their ancient culture to the end that they might develop a proud self-consciousness as a people and thus give them some incentive for striving to the end that their arid and empty acres should be fruitful. I know this is a dream for the reason that the modern world would not allow it but it is not so foolish as it may sound.[20]

At this point the romantic and realist in Neihardt seem to have clashed, although his suggestion may be interpreted to coincide with the philosophy of the Indian Reorganization Act developed by the Bureau of Indian Affairs during the administration of John Collier (1933–1945).

No doubt Black Elk felt the sense of despair that Neihardt attributes to him in *Black Elk Speaks*. He had given up his traditional religion about 1900. At that time, he told Neihardt, he was supposed to have implemented the destructive powers of his vision — powers that would wipe out the enemy, men, women, and children. He said that such a prospect made him sad, so he converted to Roman Catholicism and soon became a catechist. Like Neihardt, Black Elk was also a realist. "My children," he told Neihardt, "have to live in this world." At the time that Black Elk and Neihardt met, he had not practiced his native healing rituals nor used any of his vision powers for thirty years. He had told no one of them. His old friend Standing Bear and his son Ben heard the story of the great vision for the first time as Black Elk related it to Neihardt.

[20]Shorthand draft in the Neihardt Collection.

Black Elk Speaks is a magnificently empathetic book. It opens Black Elk's innermost life for public inspection and at the same time maintains an overriding sense of dignity. Its success is surely due in large part to Neihardt's empathetic appreciation of Black Elk's "other worldliness" — a spiritual quality that set him apart. The mystic in Neihardt and the mystic in Black Elk were kindred souls. Just as importantly, Neihardt seems to have gone to Black Elk without preconceptions. He let Black Elk create his own world, drawing the boundaries and features of his cultural landscape. Neihardt had an intuitive appreciation and understanding for other modes of thought, something akin to the modern anthropological concept of culture. And he had the gift of translating between cultures. As he wrote to House, regarding Black Elk's vision: "If it were literature instead of a dance ritual, it would be a literary masterpiece."[21]

Black Elk Speaks is a masterpiece of translating Lakota culture, within its own context, into terms understandable by readers of any culture. The book never steps outside of Lakota culture; objects in the white man's world are presented from Black Elk's perspective and called by names that reflect Lakota concepts. If the book is to be criticized, it would be for portraying Black Elk as more aloof and cut off from the real world than he actually was. At the time of his meeting with Neihardt, Black Elk's thirty-year career as a Roman Catholic may have seemed less meaningful than his earlier life. But this period in Black Elk's life related to a level of reality that lay outside of Neihardt's concern. And to Black Elk himself, his experiences as a catechist were not part of the story he wanted Neihardt to record. Today Black Elk's Catholicism presents the biggest gap in our understanding of him as a whole human being. How was it that a nineteenth-century Lakota mystic lived a full half of the twentieth century on the Pine Ridge Reservation in harmony with the encroaching white man's world?

The enthusiasm of his experience with Black Elk carried Neihardt through the writing of the *Song of the Messiah* from 1932–1935. He was immersed in the Ghost Dance era, and suffered with the power and tragic beauty of the tale. During the summer of 1934 he took

[21]Letter to House, June 3, 1931.

his daughters once again to Pine Ridge, to camp near Black Elk's place, and to explore the area of the Wounded Knee massacre as he wrote the final portions of the poem. That fall he wrote to Ben Black Elk: "I have been working steadily on 'The Song of the Messiah' and am very happy about it. I think I have never done anything half as good." He wrote into the poem the universal power for the good, the optimistic humanistic drive that motivated all his work.[22]

The poem begins by describing the bleakness of the earth, a cosmic reflection of the Lakotas' loss of their traditional world. The people are in despair; with the disappearance of the buffalo and the establishment of a reservation, all they have held sacred has come to an end. Into the confusion of their new world comes word of a Messiah, an Indian savior — Christ reincarnated. The people are quick to believe, some out of desperation, some out of true belief, some for political ends. The promise of the Messiah is no less than a new earth, rich with buffalo and populated by the living spirits of the dead, come to join the living in an Indian millenium. The means to bring about the transformation is participation in the ritual of the Ghost Dance.

The beauty of the new world to come is represented by Black Elk's vision. Neihardt weaves in material from Black Elk's Ghost Dance vision to define the highest hopes of the ghost dancers, and to generalize their millenium to all peoples. The vision is related in the third person, told by the poet-narrator:

> Below him, vivid in the glowing air,
> A young earth blossomed with eternal spring;
> And in the midst thereof a sacred ring
> Of people throve in brotherly content;
>
> . . . . . .
>
> The place was holy with the Tree that stood
> Earth-rooted yonder.[23]

This vision of salvation is offered to the Lakotas, but its realization is rendered impossible by the unbending opposition of the whites.

The central figure of *The Song of the Messiah* is Sitanka (Big Foot), the chief of the Lakotas who were killed at Wounded Knee.

---

[22]Shorthand draft in the Neihardt Collection.

[23]*The Song of the Messiah* (New York: The Macmillan Company, 1935), p. 52.

Through his participation in the Ghost Dance, Sitanka has come to realize the oneness of humankind and the joy of universal harmony, "The secret that all the Springs have tried to say," the culmination of human history. Though this cosmic harmony was not yet to be fulfilled, Sitanka half rises from his sick bed to reach out to a white soldier in whom the chief recognizes the beauty of common humanity, "The shining face, unutterably dear," radiant with the "white light" of mystic understanding . As the soldier raises his gun and brings the butt crashing down on the skull of the helpless chief, Sitanka "strove to rise in vain, To cry 'My brother!'" The defeat is a mutual one, the defeated Lakotas and the victorious whites, "Triumphant in the blindness to defeat." The poem ends with an image of the cleansing blizzard that broke after the massacre:

> All night it swept
> The bloody field of victory that kept
> The secret of the Everlasting Word.[24]

In that ultimate understanding that the poet shares with his fictional historical recreation of Sitanka and with his very real friend and teacher Black Elk, Neihardt overcomes the petty differences that separate Indians from whites. As the culmination of *A Cycle of the West, The Song of the Messiah* celebrates the triumph of the westward expansion of Europeans in the new world, but at the same time it celebrates the native sacrifice that was its inexorable consequence. For the poet, real triumph is only reached reflectively through the mystical recognition of the power of the common human spirit. Not easily expressed in words, the message transcends culture, space, and time.

The Song of the Messiah is in some ways a synthesis of the message of *Black Elk Speaks.* The latter is simpler, more direct: the story of one man's tragedy reflecting the fate of a whole people. The *Song,* on the other hand, is both the failure of humanity writ large and its ultimate triumph. Each of us is only human, pathetically manipulating our lives, unable to understand the simplest truths that both

---

[24]Ibid., pp. 108–10. My analysis is liberally borrowed from Aly, *John G. Neihardt*, pp. 183–90.

underlie and obviate our struggles. Culture becomes a barrier to understanding rather than its means.

With the publication of *The Song of the Messiah* in 1935, Neihardt turned to *The Song of Jed Smith*, the final volume of the *Cycle* to be written, and completed it in 1941. Although Neihardt did not return to Pine Ridge during these years, he did not lose touch with Black Elk. Letters occasionally passed between them. One that has survived suggests the warmth of the relationship:

Oglala, S.D.
Dec. 16, 1940

Dear Son:

Well you'll be surprised to hear from you [sic] because I dont know why you never write to me but I still remember you folks so here I am writing to you and your family. First of all I will say we're all getting along fine even up to Ben & his family. Well the weather is pretty cold up here but quite a few snow. For 5 yrs successive Ive been to the Bl[ack] Hills for the summer & pretty busy putting up a show for Duhamels[25] so I really forget to write to my friends.

Well theres [not] any news except that we're hearing about the war all the time. I hope you enjoy your holidays and may the Great Spirit bring lots of blessings.

I'm yours truly father
Nick Black Elk Sr.
Oglala S. D.[26]

The war years were lean times for Neihardt that finally brought him to Chicago and to a job with the Indian Bureau, from 1944–1945, as Director of the Bureau of Information. In this capacity, Neihardt again had the opportunity to visit Pine Ridge during the winter of 1944. His assignment was to collect material for a cultural history of the Oglalas. He intended to interview some of the old

---

[25]Duhamel's Sioux Indian Pageant at Sitting Bull Crystal Caverns, a tourist attraction south of Rapid City, South Dakota. The pageant was a serious attempt to portray Lakota culture for the purpose of educating and entertaining visitors to the Black Hills.

[26]Neihardt Collection.

women as well as men. He wrote, "They *know* something men don't know, & maybe I can get them to speak out."[27] Although this was not to be, the trip was nonetheless a marvelously productive one. Accompanied by his daughter Hilda, Neihardt arrived at Pine Ridge late in November, 1944; they were lodged at the Agency Club. For four days, November 27–29 and December 1, they interviewed Eagle Elk, one of the oldest of the traditional Oglalas then alive. He was living in a small tent next to his daughter's house at Pine Ridge. Neihardt's letter to his wife on November 29, 1944, gives a dramatic account of these meetings:

> We are working in that small tent yet & can't get old Eagle Elk to leave it. He says he'd feel strange anywhere else. It makes the old man happy to remember & tell of old times. He is truly *ancient*, & both Hiddy [Hilda] & I are fond of him. Today he told in detail all about the time he danced the Sun Dance — three days & two nights. All his tale about his foray against the Crows — with Kicking Bear & two others was merely the prelude to the sun dance, which was his dedication of himself to the service of his people and the Great Spirit. Incidentally, he told of a quirt (riding whip made of buffalo hide) which was presented to him by the one in charge of the dance after it was over. This quirt was never to be lost or given away. He must keep it always with him as a spiritual protection against all troubles, including arrows and bullets in battle. He *did* keep it all his long life until his wife died. Then when she was dead he slipped it down inside her dress against her bosom, & it was buried with her to have it for protection in her journey to the spirit world.
>
> Hiddy enjoys the talks a lot and does a wonderful job of copying on the typewriter *direct* without taking notes. This saves time.
>
> Old Standing Bear's rheumatism came back with the winter weather, & so he can't go on, but I have an even better interpreter, Billy Bergen, a man of my own age, who is quick & jolly & very able. . . . Bergen will carry on with Eagle Elk. We intend now to take his story from his earliest memory as a little boy, as he is a typical *common* Indian who experienced all the old life. This gives us a span of 90 years as he is 93. . . .
>
> I asked Eagle Elk how he thinks about the next life, when he spoke of going away any time, & he said he would be going on a long visit to his relatives. I asked him if he ever saw them, & he said sometimes he could see them dim like and whenever he did something important was always just about to happen.[28]

[27] Aly, p, 241.
[28] Photostatic copy in the Neihardt Collection.

It is unknown why Neihardt did not continue with his plan to interview a number of other older men and women. Perhaps the winter weather would not allow the necessary travel, or perhaps the cooperation was not forthcoming. In any case, Neihardt turned once again to his Indian father, Black Elk, who provided him with information he likely could not have gotten from anyone else. During seven days of interviews, December 5–8 and 11–13, Black Elk related to Neihardt a history of the Lakota people from his perspective. From a white man's perspective this history is myth, a series of non-chronological anecdotes full of mystical happenings. But from the Lakota framework within which Lakota culture developed and flourished, it is sacred history. Beginning with the dispersion of the seven bands of the Lakotas and the naming of the directions, animals, and other features of the world, the narrative discusses the introduction of the bow and arrow, fire, the knife, and the establishment of relationship among the people — the basis for the Lakota social order. Next came the prophecies of the first chief, then the actual dispersion of bands. The domestication of dogs, the creation of the political system and the details of its functioning, and the visions of Wooden Cup (called Drinks Water in *Black Elk Speaks*) that prophesied the coming of the white men and their eventual overruning of the Lakota people are each discussed in turn. Supplementing this history, Black Elk related a long traditional myth of the kind the Lakotas believe should only be told during the winter, as well as other stories of war and hunting.[29]

From these interviews another aspect of Black Elk's personality emerges. He seems less aloof and more a part of his society. Rather than the sad, defeated old man of *Black Elk Speaks*, he seems vibrant and strong, a proud preservor of the cultural traditions of his people. In these interviews Black Elk's own visions and powers are never mentioned; this is public material, the tribal legacy.

In addition to these interviews with Eagle Elk and Black Elk, Neihardt recorded only one other. On December 11 he interviewed

---

[29]The original interview notes are in the Neihardt Collection and are printed in DeMallie, ed., *The Sixth Grandfather*.

Andrew Knife who told him a longer version of a tale also related by Black Elk.[30]

Neihardt returned twice more in the interests of the Bureau of Indian Affairs. The first was for the great Sioux Victory Celebration on September 15, 1945, marking the end of World War II. Neihardt made a speech to the gathering in behalf of the Bureau. On October 11, 1945, Black Elk wrote to Neihardt to express the Indians' appreciation: "The Sioux sure liked the way you gave that speech at that celebration. They sure felt lot of encouragement by you & wish you could help them more in future."[31]

Neihardt's next visit to Pine Ridge was from September 19 to October 11, 1946. Although he no longer worked for the Bureau, he was asked to undertake a general investigation of reservation conditions. Hampered by bad weather, he spent eight days driving around the districts and the remainder of the time talking to Indians and reservation personnel at Pine Ridge itself. His investigation covered education, law and order, the tribal council, and a wide variety of other topics. The experience was sobering for Neihardt, a tonic for his tendency to take a romantic view of the Indian situation. His assessment was hard and realistic. It seemed to him that the system of self-government set up under Collier's Indian Reorganization Act was not working. The tribal organization, with its council, court, and Indian police, he wrote, "struck me as having about it a faint suggestion of comic opera." He felt that the problem was not the people, but the system. In his report he wrote:

> Oglalas have as much native intelligence as the rest of us. The trouble grows out of lack of social cohesion, out of chronic need (whatever that need may be), the jealousy and bickering that chronic need generates, the habit of looking for help from the government — the whole reservation complex.
>
> The Oglalas simply are not any longer a tribe in the social sense. Their old culture is dead. They recognize no leader. They are mostly just poor

---

[30]The story is told in Neihardt's "Red Hail and the Two Suitors," *Indians At Work*, XIII (May–June 1945), pp. 6–10; and in *When The Tree Flowered: An Authentic Tale of the Old Sioux World* (New York: The Macmillan Company, 1951), chapter 12.

[31]Letter in the Neihardt Collection.

people living together in a land that cannot support them all, and laboring under psychological, social, and economic handicaps. It is not their "Indianhood," as we used to say, but their humanhood that matters.[32]

Neihardt believed that the Oglalas could not continue to exist on the Pine Ridge Reservation as they had in the past. Many had already left, and many more would have to leave, to find employment in the towns and cities. He feared that the reservation system, with its institutionalized tribal structure, merely stood in the way of the inevitable merger of the Indians into American society at large, keeping them in poverty while staving off the inevitable. Though he did not use the word, his report seems to imply the necessity of reservation termination — an assessment unpopular both then and now. Still, this was his considered opinion, an honest appraisal arrived at without self-interest. Neihardt was never one to pull his punches; surely, it was his forthrightness that gained him respect among Indian people.

Neihardt began work on *When The Tree Flowered* in 1947, although the book was not completed until 1950. In part he attempted to retell the story of the Lakotas' struggle with the whites, to make up for the popular failure of *Black Elk Speaks*. More importantly, the materials he had collected at Pine Ridge in 1944 formed a tale worth telling. He wrote to Hilda: "It's, above all, a good story, a *romance*."[33] The plot of the book stays close to the life experiences of Eagle Elk, with an emphasis on his romantic attachments. He deftly wove into the narrative details from Black Elk's life, particularly of his trip to Europe with Buffalo Bill and of his involvement with a French woman. In many ways this book presents a more human story than *Black Elk Speaks*; as a literary character, the fictionalized narrator, whom he calls "Eagle Voice," is fully developed. The book balances love, war, humor, the sacred, and pathos. In an almost incidental fashion, the narrative incorporates Black Elk's historical and mythic tales and his accounts of Lakota social and political life.

The style of the book is conversational, Neihardt portraying himself as interviewer, sitting in the tent with Eagle Voice, while the old man tells the story of his life and of his people. This book is more

[32]A copy of the report is in the Neihardt Collection.
[33]Aly, p. 270.

descriptive than *Black Elk Speaks*, focusing more attention on making the listener understand rather than merely setting the mood. Importantly, Eagle Voice is depicted as a very vibrant man, one who does not suffer personal defeat, and whose memories, while bittersweet, are not full of regret. The book develops the theme of the prophetic visions of Wooden Cup, who long before the whites invaded Lakota country prophesied their coming, the disappearance of the buffalo, the binding of the earth with iron bands (railroads), the destruction of the people's sacred hoop, and the imposition of little square gray houses. But, says Eagle Voice, "I think I did not believe what Wooden Cup said, for I was young and the world was new."[34]

Throughout the book, Neihardt continually evokes a bittersweet mood by corrolating the erosion of Lakota culture with Eagle Voice's own aging and the increasing confusion and disorganization of his world. When he speaks of the old customs he comments, "All this was many snows ago, before the sacred hoop was broken, and when the people still were good" (p. 32). As he remembers the passing time, the battles and troubles as well as the happy times, he says, "I did not know then that the hoop was breaking and would never come together again" (p. 223). The book gives a very personal feeling for the perspective of a man grown old that seems to reflect Neihardt's own life. By this time the *Cycle*, his life's work, was long completed. When he began writing this book he was 66, and by the time he had completed it he was nearing 70. The changes wrought in the world during his lifetime approached the magnitude of those that faced his fictional Lakota character. The personal empathy is unmistakeable.

Unlike *Black Elk Speaks*, *When The Tree Flowered* carries the story of the Lakotas beyond Wounded Knee. In the chaotic aftermath of the massacre, Eagle Voice meets the girl he loved when he was a boy— now a woman whose husband and son have been killed by the soldiers. In time the two marry, but the narrator tells us little about the details of his domestic life. Speaking directly to the author, Eagle Voice summarizes his life on the Pine Ridge Reservation: "It was a good road that we walked together, Grandson. Sometimes we were hungry,

---

[34]*When The Tree Flowered*, p. 8.

but it was a good road. Our children came to us, and when we were old, we saw our grandchildren too. It was a good road" (p. 248).

When The Tree Flowered presents the traditional Lakota culture and religion as past and gone, things to be honored and remembered in the telling. But it suggests an optimistic picture of contemporary Indian life, based on strengths inherited from the past. Perhaps it reflects Neihardt's positive outlook on the Lakotas as a people who would survive the dramatic changes in their outward cultural life. In this sense it carries forward the message of *Black Elk Speaks*, putting it in fuller social context, and reintegrating the power of the sacred into everyday life.

Neihardt's Lakota legacy shows a significant internal development. *Black Elk Speaks* is closest to his actual experiences, recorded directly, with Black Elk himself. *The Song of the Messiah* integrates the understandings derived from Black Elk into an historically accurate narrative composed mainly from written sources. *When The Tree Flowered*, though no less historical, is more literary, taking interview materials directly from Black Elk and Eagle Elk but treating them more freely, inventing in some minor way a plot structure to hold the reader and to make the information presented human and believable. Each of the works expresses the Lakotas themselves, and each expresses Neihardt; as he grew in understanding, the two perspectives became inextricably intertwined.

If Neihardt had never been interested in the Lakotas, and, particularly, if he had never talked with Black Elk and Eagle Elk, our knowledge of the old Lakota way of life would be much the poorer. We would know far less about the Lakota concept of the sacred, of visions and of the powers that rule their universe. Through his work we have an invaluable perspective, an empathetic one, based on his particular life experiences and his readiness and ability to explore the domain of the "other world." We are only now beginning to understand and appreciate to its fullest John G. Neihardt's Lakota legacy. Since his birth, a century has passed, most of which he — like his long-lived Lakota friends — lived to see himself. We honor him as he honored his aged Lakota teachers; together, the wisdom and beauty of their words have left our world greener and more fruitful. Most importantly, they have taught us that we are all word senders, striving for the same understanding — "the secret," as Neihardt told us, "that all the Springs have tried to say."

Black Elk—New World Prophet

Gretchen M. Bataille

JOHN G. NEIHARDT AND BLACK ELK are familiar names to readers of American Indian literature. *Black Elk Speaks* was for many students an introduction to the mystery of the American Indian experience. Published first in 1932 and then reissued in 1961 and more recently in 1979, *Black Elk Speaks* has become a classic in American Indian literature, perhaps unsurpassed in that genre. During the fifty years since its publication, the book has been acclaimed as literature, analyzed and sometimes rejected as autobiography, described as anthropologically accurate, and condemned as "too poetic" for an Indian's voice. Despite the permutations of criticism, the book has survived and prospered. It survives today because of the two voices within — the voice of the new world prophets Black Elk and his link with the rest of the world, John G. Neihardt.

There is in *Black Elk Speaks* all that one needs to understand the broad scope of American Indian literature. In the narrative account of Black Elk's life the reader receives American history from a Sioux or Lakota perspective. The book includes accounts of the Custer battle and the Wounded Knee incident given by a participant in both events, the Indian reaction to being rounded up by the Army and placed on reservations, and the Indian rationale for participating in Buffalo Bill's Wild West shows. The reader is also introduced to both ceremonial and everyday Oglala life during the last decades of the nineteenth

Gretchen M. Bataille is a member of the Department of English at Iowa State University in Ames, Iowa.

century and into the twentieth century. The book contains humorous stories of everyday life such as High Horse's courting adventures, but it also contains important religious rituals such as the Sun Dance and the sweat lodge ceremony. Traditional tales, songs and prayers, and an account of the evolution of stories told by parents to children are also included. The rituals of hunting and fishing add a sacred quality to everyday events. The reader catches glimpses into the color symbolism when the Sacred Pipe is described, is tutored in the Sioux attitudes toward male/female relationships, and can see in Standing Bear's artwork the visual manifestation of Sioux life.

During the late sixties and early seventies *Black Elk Speaks* was a cult favorite of the young; it spoke of reverence for the earth which was part of their concern, of mysticism which attracted them, of prophecies for better times arising out of defeat and death which they wanted desperately to believe. Students loved it, read and re-read it, and were totally immersed in the "other world reality" of American Indian experience. Seldom did they question the book as autobiography. They accepted the words as "truth" and were not deterred from this interpretation even by the presence of John Neihardt's name quite obviously adorning the title page and his presence in the book itself.

The book has been received in a number of ways, and a look at its history and some predictions for its future may be in order. When *Black Elk Speaks* was first published in 1932 it was well received, but it was not a best seller. It was interesting for its story of Sioux life and was of particular interest to anthropologists and ethnologists. It remained a mildly popular book until its reissue in 1961. The times were then ready for such a book. *Black Elk Speaks* offered several messages for the counter-culture reader. The book documented in a very personal way, through the experience of one Holy Man, past treatment of the American Indians, and helped to explain the civil rights protests of the 1960's. It gave Indian activists a means of distinguishing themselves and their issues from the protests and issues of other racial minorities and was an easy reference to use when attempting to describe the life which Indians had lost because of government manipulation.

In a decade dominated by atrocities in Viet Nam, *Black Elk Speaks* portrayed yet another example of American imperialism and callousness. For another segment of American protestors it was a plea for conservation of natural resources and proof of the symbiotic relationship between human beings and the natural world. Against a backdrop of war and protest the book provided a statement denouncing materialism and extolling religious mysticism. The book was reissued just at the time when interest in ethnicity and American policies toward colored minorities was at a peak. Neihardt had, of course, presented similar arguments in his poetry, but in the person of Black Elk the case was made more effectively. In *The Song of the Indian Wars* Neihardt had shown that the Indians had retained their spiritual truths and values even though the land had been lost, and he criticized the materialistic attitudes of the whites who did not have the close relationship with nature that he recognized in the American Indians' affinity with the earth. Black Elk personalized these arguments and provided readers with a specific individual, a locale, and a time in history with which to identify.

By the 1970's literary critics had also discovered *Black Elk Speaks* and a number of articles appeared analyzing the book as literature, as autobiography, as psychology and as history. John G. Neihardt's appearance on the Dick Cavett show heightened popular interest in Black Elk's autobiography. During the 1970's there were a number of reversals in the attitudes of whites toward the ethnic minorities, changes which were apparent in popular culture portrayals in books and movies. *Little Big Man* and *A Man Called Horse*, both movies dealing with Indians of previous centuries, provided visual images which contradicted the old stereotypes and made figures such as Black Elk more credible.

In the 1980's there are many more American Indian writers publishing autobiographies, novels, poetry, and making movies. Young writers such as Leslie Silko, James Welch, and Ray Young Bear provide additional evidence to support the visionary experiences recounted by Black Elk, but at the same time political and religious conservative trends in American society threaten to eliminate anything different from mainstream values and beliefs. Fundamental religious beliefs of western people often exclude mysticism rooted in non-western value systems and traditions.

Although the book is usually classified and discussed as an autobiography, a life story told by the writer, John Neihardt makes no
such claim. In the 1961 reissue of the book Neihardt requested that
the title page read "told through" John G. Neihardt. To determine
its authenticity as autobiography critics have compared the book to
field notes taken by Neihardt's daughters during the conversations
held in 1930 and to ethnological studies of the Sioux. But autobiography is always problemmatical, and categorization is never neat.
Autobiography melds history and literature, combines objective facts
and subjective interpretations. Life narratives are *told through*,
recorded by, edited by, and *corrected by* editors. Working with a sixty-
seven year old Oglala Sioux who did not speak English, Neihardt
cannot be faulted for whatever editorial intrusions he might have
made to tell the story of Black Elk. His additions at the beginning and
in the conclusion conveyed the spirit of Black Elk, if not always the
exact words.

Critical discussion on the authenticity of the words and sequence
of stories often overlook the point of the book and certainly miss the
value to be gained by reading the story of a life within a community,
the way Black Elk perceived his relationship to the Sioux community
of which he was an integral part. By its very nature any autobiography is elusive; it is a personal self-examination which results in self-
creation and self-regeneration. The person who appears in print is not
ever the same flesh and blood person who told or wrote the story.
Neihardt recognized this truth and in the introduction to the Pocket
Books edition of *Black Elk Speaks* he wrote,

> It was my function to translate the old man's story, not only in the factual
> sense — for it was not the facts that mattered most — but rather to recreate
> in English the mood and manner of the old man's narrative.[1]

It is this *recreation* which is significant in the analysis of the book and
the character of Black Elk.

The story, the narrative, is more important than the recounting of
a single life history. The story of Black Elk is the story of a prophet,
a man who interpreted the present in terms of the past and on the

---

[1]John G. Neihardt, "The Book That Would Not Die," *Western American Literature*, 6 (Winter 1972), p. 229.

basis of both predicted the future. Neihardt described him as "kind of a preacher." Black Elk was a man who believed in prophecy, who saw pictographs on a rock bluff which had predicted the defeat of Custer and who believed that they had been put there long ago. He saw himself as a representative of and for his people, not as a savior who would redeem them, but an ordinary mortal endowed with special gifts which would provide him with the spiritual strength to endure when others faltered or perished. Yet he was plagued with a constant gnawing doubt that he had either understood his vision improperly or not acted in proper response to it. As a prophet Black Elk can be favorably compared to other prophets of history, men and women whose place in their societies paralleled that of Black Elk in his tribe.

G. Thomas Couser describes in his study of autobiography and the prophetic mode of American autobiography the impulse of autobiographers to assume the role of prophet. His theories are appropriate to describe the story of the life of Black Elk. Black Elk in the role of prophet was no doubt on Neihardt's mind, for it was his desire to learn more about the Ghost Dance and Wovoka, the prophet of the "new religion," which took him to South Dakota to collect information for *The Song of The Messiah*. Couser writes that autobiographers tend to reflect times of crisis — religious, moral, political or philosophical.[2] Black Elk in his story responds to his memories of the crisis of Wounded Knee and to the realities of the crises posed by twentieth-century encroachments on American Indian values and lifestyles. His story is told to avert the continuing crises and to alter history in such a way as to improve the life of the Sioux people, his people, and of all people.

Couser says that the prophetic autobiography flourishes in times of crisis, when change threatens communal values or when historical development demands new modes of interpretation. All of these circumstances were present at the time Black Elk told his story to Neihardt. As autobiographer Black Elk was a representative of his Oglala Sioux community, an interpreter of the past and the present, and a shaper of the history of his people. As a shaper, he functioned

[2]G. Thomas Couser, *American Autobiography: The Prophetic Mode* (Amherst: University of Massachusetts Press, 1979), p. 3.

as a prophet. In his vision Black Elk saw himself as the sixth Grand-father, the Spirit of the Earth, and he knew his work was to be done on earth, that his power was to be used in his community and for the Sioux people. In his vision historical time ceased to exist and was replaced by mythical time of a dream world, but it was a visionary world which had implications for reality because to Black Elk it was more real than the world in which he lived: "That is the real world that is behind this one, and everything we see here is something like a shadow from the world."[3] Later he says: "I knew the real was yonder and the darkened dream of it was here" (p. 85).

Couser recognizes the importance of vision to a prophet:

> ...for the anthropologist the propeht's function is to offer society a vision or a visionary experience which revises the culture's traditional myth-ology in such a way as to resolve communal crises. . . . If his vision gains credence . . . it may . . . create an illusion of change and thus bring relief by easing psychological tensions.[4]

The vision of Wovoka which initiated the Ghost Dance, the vision of Ghost Shirts to protect the wearers, and the visions recounted by Black Elk all served to ease the psychological tensions introduced by the influx of the wasichus and provided hope for the future. It is this function which Black Elk served in the recitation of his life story. In the narrative he offered his vision to the world beyond the Sioux reservation; he offered a hope for a better future for the greater com-munity. The rain which fell on Neihardt and Black Elk on the top of Harney Peak confirmed the vision and offered hope for the next ascent.

In *Black Elk Speaks* the reader learns to appreciate Indian cere-mony as drama. The initial setting for the telling of the life story is like that of Greek drama, with Black Elk as the main actor and his friends Standing Bear, Fire Thunder, and Iron Hawk acting as a chorus, reiterating the significance of certain events, explaining the context, or providing asides that Black Elk would not feel free to share. The storyteller's pauses to nap were brief intermissions, no doubt designed to give the major performer time to rest, but also to allow what had been presented to the audience time to be absorbed

---

[3]*Black Elk Speaks* (Lincoln: University of Nebraska Press, 1961), p. 85.
[4]Couser, p. 197.

and understood. The most obvious presentation of drama, however, comes during the ceremonies themselves.

Neihardt provides a hint that he saw the elements of classical drama re-enacted on the South Dakota plains. He writes, "Truth comes into this world with two faces. One is sad with suffering, and the other laughs; but it is the same face, laughing or weeping" (p. 192–93). He is describing the two masks of reality, life acted out as it is in ceremony and ritual, the raw material of drama. Black Elk tells of the *heyoka* ceremonies and the reader can easily identify the dramatic principles at work. The ceremony is acted out in a theatre of the round with an audience who at times become a chorus, commenting and reacting to the performance. The performers are costumed and acting out a ritual which is familiar, yet it is created anew each time it is performed. The pageantry is enhanced by special props, color and animals. When the end of the ceremony comes, the people are renewed. Black Elk describes the audience: "They were better able now to see the greenness of the world, the wideness of the sacred day, the colors of the earth, and to set these in their minds." (p. 197).

The dramatic re-enactment of the vision provided a catharsis and in the imitation of nature art was created, a dramatic production which portrayed the traditional symbols of Sioux culture in a new way. The horses, the four directions, the lightning, and the sacred bows were all familiar Sioux symbols, but they were given new meaning in Black Elk's vision and in the ceremonies which recreated that vision.

The continuation of the vision and of the prophet's message was ensured by the dramatic presentation during Black Elk's youth, by its retelling in 1931, and by the publication of Neihardt's book. In 1972 Neihardt wrote, "The old prophet's wish that I bring his message to the world is actually being fulfilled."[5]

Neihardt believed that a writer was a seer or a prophet, "the man who can realize the ideal without idealizing the real."[6] In his address to the Nebraska Legislature on June 18, 1921, after being named Poet Laureate of Nebraska, Neihardt said, "It must be made possible for

[5]"The Book That Would Not Die," p. 229.

[6]Blair Whitney, *John G. Neihardt* (Boston: G. K. Hall, 1976), p. 25.

the one to live vicariously the life of the many from the beginning."[7]
Certainly his writing reflected this belief. In his short story "The
Singer of the Ache," the main character Moon-Walker sees a vision
which tells him that he will be a poet and a singer. His desire to sing
of beauty and love takes him away from the activities he is expected
to perform within the community. Although he attempts to settle
down with a wife and family, he fails because his drive to sing is so
great. Finally the need to sing overwhelms him. The vision triumphs,
and through his songs Moon-Walker brings peace and solace to the
people. Moon-Walker is like Neihardt; he is also like Black Elk.
Through songs and stories both communicate with the people.
Both Neihardt and Black Elk were dreamers and visionaries, and as
Black Elk told Neihardt, "Sometimes dreams are wiser than waking"
(p. 10).

In his vision Black Elk gave his people life. In his later years he
felt that he had failed, but perhaps Black Elk has misinterpreted the
prophecy for his own life. By keeping their traditions alive, the people
continue to live. Through the telling of his life story, Black Elk
fulfilled his vision. He had performed the ceremonies and he had
recreated them now in words which would immortalize them. John
Neihardt was the amanuensis who made it possible.

[7]Quoted in Whitney, p. 29.

Nicolaus Black Elk: Holy Man in History

Roger Dunsmore

WHEN JOHN G. NEIHARDT FOUND HIM in 1930, Nicolaus Black Elk was living at the end of a dirt road in a square house with weeds growing out of the roof — an old man going blind and wondering about the great vision of his youth:

> And now when I look about me upon my people in despair, I feel like crying and I wish my vision could have been given to a man more worthy. I wonder why it came to me, a pitiful old man who can do nothing. Men and women and children I have cured of sickness with the power the vision gave me; but my nation I could not help.[1]

More than any other deed, the annihilation of Big Foot's band near Wounded Knee Creek late in December of 1890 made clear just how thoroughly the whites intended to destroy Black Elk's nation. Wounded Knee was not simply belated revenge for Custer's death;[2] it made clear that the Lakota had no recourse either in the institutions of this world or the powers of the other world. The Ghost Dance

Roger Dunsmore is a published poet and teaches American Indian Literature in the Humanities, Wilderness, and Environmental Studies Program at the University of Montana in Missoula.

[1]*Black Elk Speaks* (Lincoln: University of Nebraska Press, 1961), p. 184.

[2]The Wounded Knee slaughter was much more than just another example of a well-supplied army unit killing a band of Indians composed primarily of women, children and old men. It was an act of revenge by Custer's old outfit, the Seventh Cavalry, waiting fourteen years since the Little Big Horn to get even with the Lakota. The President of the United States presented twenty-six Medals of Honor to the men of the Seventh Cavalry for their "bravery" at Wounded Knee Creek.

which precipitated the Wounded Knee massacre was a manifestation of the desperate hope that the bison would return and the world would finally right itself by a people who had little remaining except that hope. Wovoka, the Indian prophet of the Ghost Dance, had said that

> there was another world coming, just like a cloud. It would come in a whirlwind out of the west and would crush everything in this world, which was old and dying. In that other world there was plenty of meat, just like old times; and in that world all the dead Indians were alive, and all the bison that had ever been killed were roaming around again.[3]

The hope that the white people would disappear, the belief that the old world would be renewed in familiar terms: it was for the desperate expression of these hopes and beliefs that the Lakota were punished by the United States Army. They were to be denied much more than their lands and religion and bison. The U.S. government wished to deny them the very memory of the old ways of life.

It took a while for the Sioux to realize how much they had lost, but this realization played a large part in the forty years of wondering at the end of the dead-end road to Nicolaus Black Elk's cabin: 1890–1930 — forty years when "little else but weather ever happened."

What does it mean to one who has received a great vision to protect and renew the life of one's nation in this kind of time? How might one understand the ease with which it was all swept away, that which had seemed so real and beautiful, that for which one had been made responsible? What could it possibly mean to be a man of vision in the midst of all that? Nicolaus Black Elk felt he was only a pitiful old man who was too weak to use the mighty vision that was given to him — so he gave the vision away to John Neihardt "to save his Great Vision for man." He believed in the vision after everything else was gone: somehow the vision must go on. Although he didn't understand how his vision and its power could be released in the world, still he insisted: "But if the vision was true and mighty, as I know, it is true and mighty yet; for such things are of the spirit, and it is in the darkness of their eyes that men get lost" (p. 2).

How are we to understand Black Elk? As a warrior and hunter, one of the last generation to experience the old way of life on the

---

[3]*Black Elk Speaks*, p. 237.

plains before the bison were gone? As a scout for the U.S. Army and
a performing Indian in Buffalo Bill Cody's Wild West circus at
Madison Square Garden and in European arenas? Are we to take him
as Hehaka Sapa, the shaman and visionary, and the last surviving
Oglala to have received orally the sacred rites of his nation, those
handed down to him by Elk Hand, the former "keeper of the pipe"?
Or as Nicolaus Black Elk who was so fervent a Catholic catechist that
for many years he went around trying to convert his fellow tribesmen
and who, after the publication of *Black Elk Speaks*, is claimed to have
"made in English and in Sioux formal statements of his Catholic faith,
signing them before witnesses lest he should be regarded still as
a pagan"?[4]

When we consider Black Elk's many identities and roles it becomes
clear that it is not nearly enough to take him only in his role as a
Holy Man of the Oglala. That is a beautiful and moving story, but it
avoids considering what sense, if any, he made out of the disastrous
encounter between his culture and the invading white culture. In fact,
Black Elk, even as a Holy Man, a man of vision, was so changed by
the historical terror he experienced that he ended up giving away to
the whites everything that was most sacred in his own life and in the
life of the tribe. *But* it is just this survival amidst a radical cultural
and personal dislocation that gives him his strength and makes him
important to us. If we take him as a paradigm of what it means to be
a man of vision, he revises our expectation that the holy man arrives
somewhere at the *Truth*, a truth which is recognizable to him and
to us. Instead, Black Elk is deeply involved in not knowing, and
confronts the risk that when he gives his vision away it will be ignored,
misunderstood, or misused.

It is clear that during his lifetime almost no white person heard
Black Elk's voice. *Black Elk Speaks* did not sell well, the first edition
was remaindered, and the book went out of print quickly. In 1947,
fifteen years later, another white man, Joseph Epes Brown, found
Black Elk partly crippled, almost completely blind, dressed in poor,
cast-off clothing, living in an old canvas wall tent on a Nebraska farm
where his family was working as potato pickers; a far cry from the

---

[4]*Letter*, October, 1940, Father Joseph A. Zimmerman, quoted in the publication of the Holy Rosary Mission, Pine Ridge Reservation, 1940.

perfectly enlightened, sun-tanned gurus proclaiming Truth in the Astrodome.

His life story tells us, then, that it is not enough merely to have had a great vision. A great vision is only a beginning, a starting place or point of departure, not an end, not final.

> As I lay here thinking of my vision, I could see it all again and feel the meaning with a part of me like a strange power glowing in my body; but when the part of me that talks would try to make words for the meaning, it would be like fog and get away from me.

> I am sure now that I was then too young to understand it all, and that I only felt it. It was the pictures I remembered and the words that went with them; for nothing I have ever seen with my eyes was so clear and bright as what my vision showed me; and no words that I have ever heard with my ears were like the words I heard. I did not have to remember these things; they have remembered themselves all these years. It was as I grew older that the meanings came clearer and clearer out of the pictures and the words; and even now I know that more was shown to me than I can tell (p. 49).

From Black Elk's reflection we learn that a vision must be free to direct one's life. It must not be frozen into some static truth-form. It is equally clear that what is important is the *quality of one's response* to that vision. A person must find some understanding of it, of what is being asked of one by virtue of having received it. What matters is the whole *process* of attempting to live with, from, and in terms of one's vision, to try to realize it in history, in the concrete situation in which one finds himself. And what makes that response so powerful in Black Elk's case is that this historical process takes place under the most trying historical circumstances conceivable. While with Cody's Wild West in New York, Black Elk remembered that "after a while I got used to being there, but I was like a man who never had a vision. I felt dead and my people seemed lost" (p. 221). Later in Europe, he discovered that "all the time I was away from home across the big water, my power was gone, and I was like a dead man moving around most of the time. I could hardly remember my vision, and when I did remember, it seemed like a dim dream" (p. 235). Having a great vision insures nothing at all, not even a clear memory of the vision itself.

Once we understand this perspective, then we can appreciate Nicolaus Black Elk and his life story for their importance to us and not merely as romantic wish-fulfillment about enlightenment or the visionary experience of native people. This means that we must look at Nicolaus Black Elk's *whole life story* as his expression of what it means to be a man of vision, and not focus too narrowly on the vision experience itself.[5] We must look at the slow life-long unfolding of the vision's deeper meaning as he struggled to obey and fulfill it in an utterly intractable historical situation.

The process begins early and quietly for Black Elk: he is four years old, out playing alone, and hears someone calling him. He thinks it is his mother calling, but no one is there. This happens more than once, and always makes him afraid, so he runs home. Such a gentle beginning. His fear is curious, though it all must have seemed strange to a little boy. One is reminded of Najagneg, the Eskimo shaman who told Rasmussen that the "Silam," the inhabitant or soul of the universe, is never seen; its voice alone is heard. "All we know is that it has a gentle voice like a woman, a voice so fine and gentle that even children cannot become afraid. What it says is *si la ersinarsinivdluge,* 'be not afraid of the universe.'"[6] Such a voice comes to Black Elk, a voice like his mother's, yet a frightening voice.

The next spring when he is five and out with his first bow and arrows, made for him by his grandfather, he gets a clearer experience of this voice. He is about to shoot a kingbird when it speaks to him. This intense experience of the natural world is among Black Elk's most vivid memories of the beginning of his conscious life. He did not need to go on a vision quest: the sacred powers of the universe made themselves known to him. One might say that Black Elk is one who is sought out by these powers. He does not seek them out: this fact is central to Black Elk's role as a holy man. He is still afraid; as a holy man he will no longer belong to himself, but to his vision and to his nation through his vision.

In the years after the kingbird speaks, voices come back now and then when Black Elk is alone, but he doesn't understand what they

[5] This idea from a conversation with Joseph Epes Brown.

[6] Knud Rasmussen, *Intellectual Culture of the Iglulik Eskimos* (Copenhagen: Gyldendalske Boghandel, Nordisk Forlag, 1929).

want of him, so he tries to forget them. But the summer he is nine,[7] as he is eating with Man Hip, the voices announce very clearly: "It is time; now they are calling you" (p. 21). The next day Black Elk becomes very sick with swollen arms, legs, and face. Two men from the clouds come to him in his vision and he gets up to follow them and takes a journey into the sky on a small cloud. To all outward appearances the young Black Elk lies unconscious for twelve days and his parents ask a holy man named Whirlwind Chaser to cure him.

Those twelve days of apparent coma are filled with dramatic events for Black Elk. He is summoned to a council of the Six Grandfathers: the powers of the earth and sky, and of the west, the north, the east and the south, the six powers of the world. He is taken to "the high and lonely center of the earth" so that he can see and understand. He is given the power to make live, the power to destroy, the power to heal the sick, the power to sustain his nation, the power to make peace, and the power to understand. He is called "younger brother" by the powers of the world, told that he is their relative and that "all wings of the air shall come to you, and they and the winds and the stars shall be like relatives." He is given a view of four generations in the life of his nation, including the generation that will go through cultural annihilation.

The vision also includes the whole sky full of horses. Black Elk "makes over" a faded brownish-black horse who turns out to be a big, shiny, black stallion, chief of all the horses, who sings a song that fills the universe:

> so beautiful that nothing anywhere could keep from dancing . . . the leaves on the trees, the grasses on the hills and in the valleys, the waters in the creeks and in the rivers and the lakes, the four-legged and the two-legged and the wings of the air — all danced together to the music of the stallion's songs (pp. 41–42).

[7] It is always summer when he is in direct contact with his vision. Summer is the time of intense storms on the Great Plains, with thunder and lightning, sudden winds, and rain. In fact, Black Elk likens his vision, and visions in general, to the energy of storms with their calm, fertile aftermath: "When a vision comes from the thunder beings of the west, it comes with terror like a thunder storm; but when the storm of vision has passed, the world is greener and happier; for wherever the truth of vision comes upon the world, it is like a rain. The world, you see, is happier after the terror of the storm" (p. 192).

In short, Black Elk receives a powerful vision of the true community of all beings. He is shown his true relationship to everything, including the very powers of the world, and he is given the power and responsibility to care for his own nation in the midst of a terrible future. The vision is all unsought, given to a nine-year-old boy whose initial response to it is fear that if he tells anyone about it they won't believe him, youngster that he is. Though he can feel the meaning of it "like a strange power glowing in my body," and old Whirlwind Chaser can "see a power like a light all through his body," the young Black Elk is afraid the people will think that he is crazy and so he hides from Whirlwind Chaser (pp. 48–50).

The experience of the vision leaves an indelible impression and for twelve days following it he wants to be alone and feels that he doesn't belong to his people. During this time when he is out with the bow and arrows his grandfather made for him, he starts thinking about his vision and feels strange. He tries to forget about it by shooting a small bird sitting in a bush. Just as he is going to shoot he feels strange again, remembering that "I was to be like a relative with birds," so he doesn't shoot it. Then he feels foolish about that, and so kills a green frog by a creek but is upset immediately.

It is clear that he will never be the same again. He will not take his relationships to other creatures lightly. Still, by mid-summer he manages to quit thinking about his vision and in the following years there is much to distract him. Bison hunting, storytelling, the movement of whites into Lakota country with Custer's discovery of gold in the Black Hills in 1874, a big Sun Dance, Crazy Horse's defeat of General Crook on the Rosebud, the defeat of Custer on the Little Big Horn, the murder of Crazy Horse and the band's flight into Canada: all these events occur in quick succession. The band finally returns to their own country in the spring of 1879 when Black Elk is sixteen.

During those eight years (1872–80) of trauma for the Lakota, Black Elk seems to forget his vision and the powers he has received from it. At times he does receive help in finding game and in horse racing. He has protection while fighting, premonitions that something terrible is about to happen, and always has a continuing sense of other creatures as sacred. Although the vision is hidden from others and largely forgotten, it is there at critical moments supporting and reminding him. Yet as he sees his nation being torn apart by warfare and undermined by the lies of corrupted chiefs such as Spotted Tail, he wonders if maybe his vision was only a queer dream after all.

After Crazy Horse is murdered and Black Elk's family flees to Canada, the vision begins to press him more as the desperate circumstances of his people become clearer. He begins to wonder when his "duty is to come." His description of his emotional confusion just prior to his first public relevation of his vision shows us the increasing tension he was experiencing:

> A terrible time began for me then, and I could not tell anybody, not even my father and mother. I was afraid to see a cloud coming up; and whenever one did, I could hear the thunder beings calling to me: "Behold your Grandfathers! Make haste!" I could understand the birds when they sang, and they were always saying: "It is time! It is time!" The crows in the day and the coyotes at night all called and called to me: "It is time! It is time!"
>
> Time to do what? I did not know. Whenever I awoke before daybreak and went out of the tepee because I was afraid of the stillness when everyone was sleeping, there were many low voices talking together in the east, and the daybreak star would sing this song in the silence:
>
> > "In a sacred manner you shall walk!
> > Your Nation shall behold you!"
>
> I could not get along with people now, and I would take my horse and go far out from camp alone and compare everything on the earth and in the sky with my vision. Crows would see me and shout to each other as though they were making fun of me: "Behold him! Behold him!"
>
> When the frosts began I was glad, because there would not be any more thunder storms for a long while, and I was more and more afraid of them all the time, for always there would be the voices crying: "Oo oohey! It is time! It is time!"
>
> The fear was not so great all the while in the winter, but sometimes it was bad. Sometimes the crying of coyotes out in the cold made me so afraid that I would run out of the one tepee into another, and I would do this until I was worn out and fell asleep. I wondered if maybe I was only crazy; and my father and mother worried a great deal about me (pp. 163–64).

Finally his parents asked an old holy man, Black Road, to try to cure him. Black Elk's fear compelled him to tell the old man the visions, experiences, and turmoil that he had been carrying inside himself for eight years. "You must do your duty and perform this vision for your people upon earth," Black Road told him and added that if he failed to do his duty something very bad would happen to him.

From this account it is clear that to be a man of vision is, first of all, to be a man of duty. And the first duty to one's vision is to share it, not simply with an elder holy man, but also with one's people. To share the vision will release a person, and it will also release the power of the vision into the life of the people. The very first act of letting go, of sharing, will eventually take the man of vision beyond his own culture. Not to share this vision and to contain within oneself all that one has received is to turn the vision against oneself and to rob one's people of its benefits.

And so Black Road and another elder named Bear Sings help the seventeen-year-old Black Elk dramatize that part of the vision he called the horse dance. A sacred tepee is painted with pictures from his vision. There are four black horses and four white horses, four sorrels and four buckskins, a group for each of the four great directions, each horse with a young rider; and there are six very old men to represent the Six Grandfathers. Black Elk's vision recurs as the people re-enact it. Even the thunder beings attended the performance: rain and hail fall and lightning flashes just a short distance from the dancers. The performance continues until everyone in the village has joined in the dancing, those without horses dancing on foot, everyone singing the vision songs together. At its conclusion Black Road offers a prayer to the Powers of the World with the pipe and passes it around *until everyone in the whole village* has smoked at least one puff. Then Black Elk's fear is gone so that he is glad to see thunder clouds and the whole band feels happier and healthier, even those people who had been sick. Sharing of the vision through song and dance brings the people and Black Elk a sense of accomplishment and contentment. Even their horses respond with an increased sense of well-being (p. 179).

Then Black Elk goes through a long winter waiting for the thunder beings to reappear in the spring so that he can do his next duty, which is to go out "lamenting" with the help of another old man, Few Tails.

This lamenting, or praying for understanding, is so that "the spirits would hear me and make clear my next duty" (p. 186). As each duty is fulfilled, another duty arises. And yet the next duty is never clear; it must be clarified with the help of the elders. One must live out the vision to learn how to use the powers bestowed. This process of gradual maturity and awareness is carefully guided by the oldest and wisest men of one's nation and is supported by the whole community through their participation in the ritual re-enactments of the vision.

The holy man has to act in history and cannot avoid the agonizing attempt to understand what is being asked of him. How can he best use his powers on earth for the people? It is this aspect of Black Elk's visionary process which seems to me to be so instructive today. Black Elk's situation seems more difficult than most, to his credit he neither becomes a fanatic, certain of the truth of his own understanding, nor does he give way to despair and hopelessness, but tries to understand how to put his vision to work in a world increasingly alien to it.

Black Elk is not one who knows but *one who has been known* by the unknown in a terrifying and astonishing way. He always lives in the edge of what he calls "the beauty and the strangeness of the earth" (p. 277). Black Elk never speaks to us as one who has experienced absolute truth but always speaks as one who has experienced the beauty and strangeness of the world. He has been astonished, terrified, bewildered by that beauty and strangeness.

Black Elk receives another vision from his lamenting, the dog vision which he decides to perform with *heyokas*, sacred clowns, to make the people laugh, for "when people are already in despair, maybe the laughing face is better for them" (p. 193). A Holy Man named Poor takes charge of this ceremony for him with Black Elk himself performing as one of the clowns. The ceremony ends with the whole community rushing to a pot where the sacrificial dog has been boiled. Everyone tries to get a piece of the sacred flesh to eat. It is a medicine to make them happier and stronger and

When the ceremony was over everybody felt a great deal better, for it had been a day of fun. They were better able now to see the greenness of the world, the wideness of the sacred day, the colors of the earth, and to set these in their minds (p. 197).

Again the effect of the ceremony is to reaffirm their sense of the unity of the world.

It is after the performance of the heyoka ceremony that Black Elk is first able to cure. He cures a small boy who has been very sick for a long time. Even so, he speaks of being *afraid* because he has never cured before, is unsure of his power, and, in fact, feels his way along as he works over the boy, pausing to think here and there until his doubts diminish and he understands better how to proceed. He tells us that he was so eager to cure this boy that he called on "every power there is" although he knew that only one power would have been sufficient.

This summer of his first cure another medicine man, Fox Belly, assisted him in performing his duty to that part of the vision that contained the power of the bison. After this ceremony he felt more confident of himself, his doubt vanished, and he felt the power within him constantly and became busy curing the sick. The next summer he engaged the wise man Running Elk to help him perform the ceremony of the elk as his duty to that part of the vision. Whirlwind Chaser, Black Road, Bear Sings, Few Tails, Poor, Fox Belly and Running Elk: these men are the elders, the carriers of the ancient wisdom, who guide and assist young Black Elk in the early stages of fulfilling his vision. They help him shape it into forms that bring it into the life of the community.

In the fall of 1883 the last of the great bison herds is slaughtered by the whites and the Lakota are settled in shacks on the reservation, wholly dependent on the government for issues of beef and flour. Black Elk continues curing for three years, but this power seems trivial in the face of his people's annihilation. "What are many little lives," he asks, "if the life of those lives be gone?" (p. 218). His despair is deep. He wishes to be able to heal the sacred hoop of his nation and not simply the lives of individuals who are sick.

In the summer of 1886 recruiters for Buffalo Bill's Wild West show come to the Lakota looking for Indians to join their troup and perform. Black Elk decides to go, motivated by the desire to see and understand the powerful world of the whites, in the hope that he will find some secret there to help him bring the sacred hoop back together again. This quest takes him to Omaha, Chicago, New York City and

across the ocean to England and France. Predictably he finds nothing
to help his people in any of these places because, as he says, the whites
had forgotten that the earth was their mother and "had even the grass
penned up:"

> I looked back on the past and recalled my people's old ways, but they
> were not living that way any more. They were traveling the black road,
> everybody for himself and with little rules of his own, as in my vision.
> I was in despair, and I even thought that if the Wasichus had a better
> way, then maybe my people should live that way (p. 219–221).

Black Elk was gone for three years, during which he nearly died,
and came back to the reservation to find things worse than ever before.
Drought, starvation, lies, the reservation reduced by a new treaty, the
people pitiful and in despair — he found only desolation. He was
now without power, like a dead man, and could barely remember his
vision. The news of the Ghost Dance reached his tribe that summer
and it was hard for him to believe. He listened all winter to accounts
of the new religion, waited and wondered. His father died. He worked
in a white man's store, puzzled, wondering if he should try to put the
power of his vision and the power of this new religion together.
The similarities seemed to be great. Finally he decided to go to a Ghost
Dance. He saw the likenesses for himself, decided to enter into the
new religion, and had new visions from which he made ghost shirts
for many others.

He told his new vision through songs, the people weeping together
for the beautiful world that had been taken from them. But eventually Black Elk came to feel misled by these new visions:

> We danced there, and another vision came to me. I saw a Flaming Rain-
> bow, like the one I had seen in my first great vision. Below the rainbow
> was a tepee of cloud. Over me there was a spotted eagle soaring, and
> he said to me: "Remember this." That was all I saw and heard.
>
> I have thought much about this since, *and I have thought that this was
> where I made my great mistake.* I had had a very great vision, and
> I should have depended only upon that to guide me to the good. But
> I followed the lesser vision . . . It is hard to follow one great vision in
> this world of darkness and of many changing shadows. Among those
> shadows men get lost (p. 253–54; emphasis added).

Even holy men of vision make mistakes and temporarily lose their vision in the historical events of their time.

When Big Foot's band is slaughtered at Wounded Knee, Black Elk wants to die also. The heaps of bodies of women and children are too much for him. Later he wants to kill and get revenge. He is badly wounded in the stomach but survives and even takes part in another skirmish two weeks later despite his wound.

Then begins the forty years of silence and desperation which ends when we hear his voice again through John Neihardt. It is no accident that Black Elk has nothing to say about the years between 1890 and 1930 because they were a long, continuous heartache. Perhaps they are too painful for him to describe. But unless we realize that from the age of 27 to the age of 67 he is frozen in a single moment of despair, we run the danger of misunderstanding him completely.

The important elements, then, of this process of attempting to understand his vision, to do his duty to it, to release its power on earth in the life of his nation, are: (1) that it was not sought — it claimed him very early in his life, (2) that his initial response to it was fear and avoidance, the attempt to forget it, (3) that not to share it with the people of his tribe was to render it destructive, to turn its energy against him, (4) that sharing it involved him in an apprenticeship to the elders in his tribe and took up everyone in the immediate band as participants, (5) that having had a vision entailed grave duties and responsibilities to his people and to the world, and (6) that having a vision in no way guaranteed a sense of personal certainty but demanded instead continuous attention to the *collective* process of unfolding its meaning and sharing that meaning with an ever-widening circle of people. This whole process, then, leads him to his final duty.

Black Elk's fundamental duty to his vision is always to seek understanding. As he says many times, "It is from understanding that power comes; and the power in the ceremony was in understanding what it meant" (p. 212). For him the path to understanding is difficult: beginning in fear at the urgency with which the voices from his vision address him: "It is time! It is time!" Fearful because he does not know how to do what they want and fearful because although he had done his duty to the various parts of the vision, nevertheless his nation had been destroyed. But only in the act of relinquishing his vision, *in giving it away*, did he understand it on the deepest level.

As long as Black Elk held his vision close in the death-grip of his own cultural tradition its power mocked him just as it mocked him when he held it locked in his own private personality and made him think he was crazy. By letting it go its own way into the world Black Elk acknowledges that the vision has a life of its own. And this life is not meant simply for him and his people but for all peoples. Strangely this independent existence of the vision has been clearly expressed as a part of the original vision itself:

> . . . I was seeing in a sacred manner the shapes of all things in the spirit, and shapes of all shapes as they must live together like one being. And I saw that the sacred hoop of my people was one of many hoops that made one circle, wide as daylight and as starlight, and in the center grew one mighty flowering tree to shelter all the children of one mother and one father. And I saw that it was holy (p. 43).

The failure of the vision to protect and renew the life of his nation serves to show Black Elk that his understanding of the vision must move beyond the limits of his own culture. It is a painful realization but it is just this honesty in the face of limits that is so compelling about Black Elk. He never doubted that what he had experienced was real and powerful and true. He never felt that his vision and the sacred powers of the world were empty because they did not save his nation from a terrible destruction. Nor did he escape from the painful historical reality of that destruction into his vision, calling it the only abiding reality and regarding the world and what happens in it insignificant by comparison. He startles us by his capacity to maintain the necessary interconnectedness between the physical, historical world and the world of sacred powers of his vision. Black Elk maintained this interconnectedness under the pressure of the greatest possible historical terror and despair.

Nicolaus Black Elk waited at his historical dead-end forty years. Wondering, slowly going blind, he never relinquished his grip on either the world or the vision until there was a way to let them both go together. The vision itself was to be twisted a bit in its transmission, printed in a foreign tongue in a book to be read by white people who had forgotten that the earth and sky and the four great directions are sacred ancestors. In giving away his vision, Black Elk completed the great circle and affirmed that we are indeed all relatives. We are at the center of the wisdom of Black Elk when we understand this relatedness of all things in the circle of life in the act of giving away.

There are four examples of giving away within Black Elk's narrative. The first two deal with giving away within the tribe; the other two extend that act to some part of the natural world. In Black Elk's account of the Sun Dance the warrior who counted coup on the tree that would be the center-pole proved his courage through his capacity to give to those in need: " . . . a warrior, who had done some very brave deed that summer, struck the tree, counting coup upon it; and when he had done this, he had to give gifts to those who had least of everything, and the braver he was, the more he gave away" (p. 96).

Giving away is always remaining within the circle and using one's power in the manner in which the power of the world works, in expressing relatedness. In preparing for the bison hunt,

> the head man of the advisors went around picking out the best hunters with the fastest horses, and to these he said: "Good young warriors, my relatives, your work I know is good. What you do is good always; so today you shall feed the helpless. Perhaps there are some old and feeble people without sins, or some who have little children and no man. You shall help these, and whatever you kill shall be theirs." This was a great honor for young men (p. 56).

Giving away was a means of affirming that all are relatives in the great hoop of the world. In another place Black Elk and his father kill two deer:

> While we were butchering and I was eating some liver, I felt sorry that we had killed these animals and thought that we ought to do something in return. So I said: "Father, should we not offer one of these to the wild things?" He looked hard at me for a while. Then he placed one of the deer with its head to the east, and, facing the west, he raised his hands and cried: "Hey-hey" four times and prayed like this: "Grandfather, the Great Spirit, behold me! To all the wild things that eat flesh, this I have offered that my people may live and the children grow up with plenty" (pp. 64–65).

Always the life of the wild things and the life of one's own children are taken together here; they are not understood as belonging to separate realms.

The knowledge of the circle informs the act of giving away. So when Black Elk gives his vision away, he gives it back to the grandfather and the great men of his tribe. In the preface of the book we read: "What is good in this book is *given back* to the six grandfathers and to the great men of my people." Black Elk pays his debt in gratitude to the natural world and to the wise men of his tribe by giving the vision away, transmitting it in the only way left to him. The logic is simple, impeccable, and rooted in the deepest tradition of his own culture. Nicolaus Black Elk's life story and the wisdom of the traditional ways of the Oglala Sioux are not merely a romantic longing for a way of life that is gone. They are, above all, the story of a *duty* of all those who have received a great vision.

Renewing the Sacred Hoop

Carl J. Starkloff, S.J.

JOHN G. NEIHARDT WAS AN EPIC POET of the old West, especially of the primeval West — the world of the American Indian. He portrayed this world with the beauty and power that it had, even as he showed to his European-American compatriots the terrible things they were doing to the natives of the land they were invading. Thus Neihardt was a tragedian describing for white Americans the death of their own innocence as noble seekers for truth and freedom. This loss of innocence was reflected in the grief and agony of those who suffered at their hands — not without incredibly harsh and often brilliantly conceived wars of resistance — as they trampled out the vintage of Manifest Destiny.

Neihardt appears to have tried consistently to be a true and accurate "phenomenologist," that is, one who observes the given phenomena without prejudice while striving to enter into the inner mind of the object he is observing. The "object" thus becomes a real *subject* for him, because he unites his intention with that of the other. In this way, Neihardt has something to show about learning cultural values and understanding persons who live them *for their own sake*. But the great poet of the West seems to have had his own blind spots. He passes over in silence, for example, the fact that Black Elk, the Lakota medicine man, was also Nicolaus Black Elk after his conversion to

Carl J. Starkloff, S. J., received his doctorate in systematic theology from the University of Ottawa and now teaches at Regis College, Toronto School of Theology in Ontario.

Catholicism in the early years of this century, and that as Nicolaus Black Elk he served as a catechist on the Pine Ridge Reservation for many years. Perhaps as a poet Neihardt was also a bit of a primitivist and a romantic. Christianity as we know it in America would certainly have introduced elements of modernity and inconsistency in the prosaic orderliness of the picture he wished to paint.

Still, I have no desire to write an "apologetic" by trying to prove whether or not Black Elk's great visions or his own interpretations of them were of Christian or Indian origin and inspiration. They might have been all of that and also simply a part of the great unconscious of a deeply holy human being. No doubt all of these elements influenced him by the time he spoke with Neihardt. A seeker of holy things, Black Elk would not have distinguished his sources in the manner in which we are accustomed. He was, I suspect, an early example of what might become a strong and healthy syncretism of symbols in the gradual development of a spiritual vision. For those of us who believe that Jesus Christ (not "Christianity," which inevitably comes to mean "Western Civilization") has the same gift of infinite value and enduring life to offer all people, a knowledge of persons like Black Elk might show us how to let the "seeds of the Word" grow slowly and gradually within a unique culture like the Lakota. Surely those for whom Black Elk is an inspiration as a true *Indian* visionary need not feel that any Christian experience he might have had in any way detracts from his primeval richness. He was who he was.

Black Elk and so many Indians like him serve as catechists to missionaries. In this role they give us occasions for sober reflection on the great tensions that they have experienced and still must confront in trying to integrate their lives around so many diverse symbols. While we should not be too hard on our predecessors who often rather barbarously assaulted the native cultures (for we are all children of our times), we can learn from their mistakes and develop our own abilities to see where native values and symbols contribute something positive, not only to Indian Christianity but to Western Christianity as well. If we bring Jesus Christ to a culture, let it not be a Christ who *negates* that culture, but the Christ of St. John's Gospel who pitches His tent among His people in order to *transform* all culture by permeating it with even more radiant light — the light of one who came not to destroy but to fulfill.[1] While Neihardt does not affirm this idea, neither does he present us with a picture of religious conflict in which Christianity and the traditional Lakota religion are opposed to each other.

We read in Neihardt's books about the broken circle, how the hoop of the Lakota nation has been shattered and how the center of the universe has been lost. But we also read how Black Elk told Neihardt that "anywhere is the center of the world."[2] This conception of centrality was a deeply spiritual insight that might have come from his own native endowment or from an authentic Christianity. The idea that the Lakota hoop was only one smaller hoop which constituted the peoples of the world is not foreign to the Lakota religion, and it is certainly not foreign to the Christian religion. It may be among the deepest insights which they share.

Christians are often rather facile in portraying their faith as a "universal" faith which stands over and against the tribal worldview of primitive peoples. But if we examine our own origins more carefully and refine our notions of tribal existence more precisely, stripping away the influence of our national and social background, it may well be asked how much universality is left to us. How free are we, truly, to accept an authentically universal Christ who relativizes all of our cultural absolutes and ideologies? The Christian missionary, it seems to me, even while he may share the insight of tribal elders (that we cannot retreat back into tradition), must still have some of the spirit of Jacques Ellul, who wrote of "the city," of modern technological civilization:

> A time comes in the periodic renewal of man's passion for the city when a Christian must pronounce the *non possumus*. Every moment in history is not the same thing. As concerns the city, we must not forget that Abraham once went to rescue the king of Sodom, and was blessed for it by Melchizedek, whereas soon after this, Lot had to flee Sodom because it had incurred the Lord's temporal wrath.[3]

[1] See H. Richard Niebuhr, *Christ and Culture* (New York: Harper and Row, 1951), especially p. 45 ff and p. 196.

[2] *Black Elk Speaks*, p. 43.

[3] Jacques Ellul, *The Meaning of the City*, trans. Dennis Pardee (Grand Rapids: Eerdmans, 1970), p. 182.

We live in constant tension between progress and primitivism, and the missionary is as easy a prey to the extremes of these positions as anyone else. In many ways, to seek to discover, or to rediscover, the values of tribal peoples is not to "go back" but to focus on enduring truths salutary to our human nature. These truths were allowed to surface in *Black Elk Speaks* and *When the Tree Flowered* because Neihardt instinctively understood that they transcended the historical experiences in which Black Elk and the other Sioux elders originally apprehended them.

The missionary, then, or the missionologist who seeks to reflect on the nature and function of mission, may have an entirely different motivation from that of Neihardt the poet. But he can learn from Neihardt's method of reproducing the highest expressions of a culture and by looking and listening and asking very simple questions. I might venture to say that many missionaries might well have spent their entire careers in such a dialogical situation without ever administering the sacraments or developing any advanced catechists or native priests, or theology or proclamation, being content only to sow the most fundamental seeds of the Gospel while they learned about the religious lives of their dialogue partners in tribal society. This service is in fact something similar to what Vincent Donovan did in East Africa, which he described in his remarkable account of his mission work on that continent:

> Suppose *you* were a missionary and you realized how questionable the whole system was? . . . Maybe you would do as we did, begin all over again from the beginning. That means precisely what it says, starting from the beginning, with, perhaps, only one conviction to guide you, a belief that Christianity is of value to the world around it. That is presumption enough. Beyond that, no preconceived ideas either as to what Christianity is or what paganism is. What it means is a willingness to search honestly for that Christianity and to be open to those pagan cultures; to bring Christianity and paganism together and see what happens, if anything happens; to see what emerges if anything can emerge, without knowing what the end result will be.[4]

This task, of course, is the theological equivalent of the poet's openness to meaning which Neihardt personified so well.

[4]Vincent J. Donovan, *Christianity Rediscovered* (Notre Dame, Indiana, Fides/Claretian, 1978), pp. 1–2.

However, since the churches did not generally move in this manner (and thus brought great numbers to baptism within a European form of Christianity, and so often into the mere shell of faith), the modern Church is still only a mission church in most areas of mission activity. Few of us today would have conceived of or attempted to do anything better, and perhaps no other approach to mission would have been any more successful had we stood in our predecessors' shoes.

In our own times, that kind of learning in the Roman Catholic Church is best exemplified in Vatican Council II, of which Karl Rahner has said that, for the first time, there was "a council precisely of the world church." It was an event introducing a third great epoch in church history: following Jewish Christianity and Hellenistic and European Christianity with the period in which the sphere of the Church's life is the entire world.[5] The Church is truly "catholic" when it takes in and includes all cultures. To take this idea seriously is to open ourselves to a revolutionary idea of the Church; it is to ask ourselves, for instance, whether the forms of local church practice in Plains Indian culture might not reflect more deeply the realities of the Sun Dance, Vision Quest, Sweat Lodge, namings, paintings, the making of relatives, and so on. It might mean, far more importantly, some different expressions of and emphases on morality. At the very least, we must be questioning the use of symbols that so often speak of a foreign power that dominates the life of a people.

But in order to approach mission activity in this way, we will have to radically change our own thinking. The missionary has to consider the "hidden motives" in his pastoral work, a pregnant phrase aptly used in the title of a book on this subject by Juan Luis Segundo. I have already alluded to the assumptions that we so easily make about the universality of Christianity. With Segundo, I would suggest further that we examine our notions of lordship as applied to Christ, and of how this is freely accepted by people. Segundo argues emphatically that people in Latin America, especially the oppressed and impoverished, have seldom been able to make a free act of Christian faith.[6]

[5]Karl Rahner, "A Basic Interpretation of Vatican II," *Theological Studies*, XL (December 1979), p. 718, trans. Leo J. O'Donovan, S. J.

[6]Juan Luis Segundo, S. J., *The Hidden Motives of Pastoral Action*, trans. John Drury (Maryknoll, N.Y.:Orbis Books, 1978), pp. 65–82.

They have either been forcibly converted, as they were in the first centuries of contact, or have adhered to the Church because it holds social and economic power. The question may be validly asked about the conversion of many native people of North America: How many of these people may have become Christians because Christianity promised some deliverance from a foreign military power under the reservation system? Indeed, the decreasing need of Indian people today to resort to such a refuge may well be the beginning of a new, more liberated and amateur allegiance to Christianity.

Power in its various forms has always been an object of the Native American religious quest. Neihardt pointed out in a tragically beautiful way the struggle of Indian people to find the power to keep from being destroyed as a people. For the Church to offer such help, often through its agreements with secular government, may have been at times historically providential and may be so again, but this kind of power is not ultimately what Jesus Christ's lordship means. Power, for the Christian, is recognized in a loving God who in His all-power *gives* Himself.[7] This self-giving is open to free acceptance or rejection by human beings. It embodies the power to change their hearts. In Jesus Christ, the powerful self-giving means, paradoxically, the surrender of power and the acceptance of the human condition. If the Church is to witness this Christ-reality, it will be through surrendering the use of worldly power for its own aggrandizement and drawing upon power as grace to serve those who are oppressed. Through such a loss and rediscovery of power — power in the Spirit — the Gospel message is proclaimed to the poor who are then called to grow toward maturity as free persons before God. If the Church is to be involved at all with secular power, it must be only in order to help remove the evils that hinder faith-existence.

The missionary must adopt as his own method of "inculturating" the gospel among native peoples an approach that bears some similarity to the inquiring attitude of John Neihardt — a humble yet burning passion to know and understand. But the missionary must have greater hope for the future and a determination to do something about it. Theologically, such a method for understanding primal

[7]On the concept of power, see G. Van der Leeuw, *Religion in Essence and Manifestation*, trans. J. E. Turner (New York: Harper and Row, 1963), p. 177.

religious experience has been set forth by Bernard Lonergan, though not explicitly as a method. The basic dynamic of this method, now well-known among theologians, is what can be of interest to us. Lonergan distinguishes between the classicist notion of culture and the empirical notion: "When the classicist notion of culture prevails, theology is conceived as a permanent achievement, and then one discusses its nature. When culture is conceived empirically, theology is known to be an ongoing process, and then one writes on its method."[8] The present danger is that this kind of methodology, to which Vatican II opened up the Church, will be destroyed by a renewed conservative reaction.

To make the theology of mission an ongoing, open-ended process, we must recognize a certain structural dynamism in the human consciousness, consisting of what Lonergan calls the four transcendental precepts: Be attentive, Be intelligent, Be reasonable, and Be responsible. This dynamism shapes the formation of all subsequent method. Inherent in the process one has an open intentionality, an in-tending, a reaching-for, towards experience, towards understanding, towards reasoning, towards eventual decision. This method, as it touches religion, thus requires constant expansion of one's horizons and makes conversion an ongoing experience of self-transcendence. Conversion in this context means "a transformation of the subject and his world," and is to be considered three ways—intellectual, moral, and religious.[9]

Intellectual conversion is continual growth in objectivity in one's view of reality. Moral conversion depends on the ability to scrutinize one's intentional response to values and to choose on the basis of value rather than feeling. Religious conversion is to be grasped by ultimate concern, actually involving a fifth transcendental precept: Be in love unconditionally. Each dimension of conversion, finally, is an aspect of the overall quality of self-transcendence.[10]

I offer this very brief summary of Lonergan's fundamental method because it can be of such immense value to one working in a "primitive" or "pagan" culture, and I do not use the word pejoratively, where

[8]Bernard J. F. Lonergan, S. J., *Method in Theology* (New York: Herder and Herder, 1972), p. xi.
[9]Ibid., p. 130.
[10]Ibid., p. 240.

knowledge of how to listen is so vital, or, as is often the case now, in the painfully complex milieu of a culture in transition and perhaps on the path of destruction.

A truly transcendental approach to such a culture will open the missionary to the depth of resources available among the people as well as to their problems. In my own experience among native cultures, for instance, I have experienced some forms of intellectual conversion, or "radical clarification" as to the uniqueness of their worldview as well as its complexity. I can no longer speak of traditional Indians as "simple people," or claim to have any ready access as a non-Indian to understanding them. Moral conversion has come to me in the form of a maturity in learning from native peoples about community, patience, suffering, and keeping things in perspective. In mutually accepting and giving challenges about morality, I have learned from them about problems of justice both locally and nationally, and undergone changes in viewpoint. Finally, I have been gifted with religious conversion in a number of ways through the rites, symbols, and guidance of the elders. But nowhere has this conversion been more pronounced than in experiencing a hitherto unfathomed "simplicity and passivity in prayer."[11]

As I have indicated, the situation is extremely complicated. Neihardt depicted the beginning of this tangle of values and worldview in his conversations with Black Elk and in his fictitious interviews with Eagle Voice where he showed the tragedy of the shattering of the sacred hoop. We now deal with an additional forty years of tribal disintegration and cultural and religious inter-mingling. There is indeed no going back to the old sacred hoop. That world, should we try to reconstruct it, would be no more than a carcass riddled with the disease of social decay, alcoholism, despair, apathy, and alienation. We need a new synthesis, the discovery of a new and more widely embracing sacred hoop that can provide inspiration to all people. This perceived need means that we walk the line between sentimental nostalgia and hard, uninspired, prosaic pragmatism. For Christian missionaries it means that they offer the unqualified love of God for all people as shown in Jesus Christ, reaching beyond all bounds of .

[11]Ibid., p. 241.

tribe or nation while they encourage native peoples who desire to be Christians to bring forth and develop their own religious heritage. They are already finding that the two sides have much in common in their authentic elements. And there is no question that Neihardt's depiction of the traditional elements of Sioux religion, as seen in *Black Elk Speaks*, has been an immeasurable help to young Native Americans seeking to incorporate the best of their tradition in this new synthesis.

One further element of the modern world needs attention here — the very difficult concept of secularization. The phenomenon has been around for as long as people have tried to distinguish between types of causality in the world. In our own era, it received its greatest exposure in the 1960's through the work of Harvey Cox, who called it "the liberation of man from religious and metaphysical tutelage, the turning of his attention away from other worlds and towards this one."[12] It entailed *the disenchantment of nature, the desacralization of politics*, and *the deconsecration of values* — all based in the Judeo-Christian heritage and pointing in Cox's view toward a more enlightened Christianity. I leave off discussing where Cox's pilgrimage has since taken him, however, and would instead indicate the devastating effect such a dynamic as secularization — which properly understood may well be an enlightened process — would have in its sudden confrontation with tribal society. Cox himself discussed this point in *The Secular City*. Whatever a healthy secularization might contribute to human growth, its application has generally been far from gentle or felicitious. But what calls for an even more careful examination is how the Church and its ministers have experienced and used the concept of secularization: it is perhaps the most badly handled of all hidden motives in pastoral work.

Theologians have often claimed that the Gospel is a secularizing dynamic in the good sense — that it frees persons from slavish adherence to tribal taboos, to religious law, to ceremony, and the like. This characterization is fair enough if, as I have said, the dynamic of liberation recognizes the true value in tribal life and religion, which is really far more "this-worldly" than most theologians ever dream. But the

[12]Harvey Cox *The Secular City* (New York: The Macmillan Company, 1966), p. 17.

more significant point for Christians in relation to native peoples, especially in the United States, lies in the thinly-veiled, anti-prophetic identification of the churches with various forms of civil religion, often under the appearance of separation of church and state. With Segundo, who finds Latin Americans unable to accept any kind of secularization process, I would question whether Europeans or North American whites (especially those who profess any form of Christianity) find it very congenial either.[13]

We think we are free of tribal viewpoints, taboos, rituals, burdensome religious law, and so on. What we have often done, however, is to employ or work with the power of the state to bring Indian people not Christianity, but what amounts to a white person's tribal religion. We have secularized primal society while failing to recognize our own complicity in a more subtle form of the sacral state as it enshrines Euro-American values, symbols, laws, and customs. Small wonder that even those whole-hearted Indian converts to Christianity have phrased their conversion as: "I chose to go the white man's way!" There will be a deepening of church efforts among native peoples only as the Church recognizes its own tribal elements and appreciates those of its newer adherents. This deepening does not mean unquestioning acceptance on anyone's part: all must challenge one another if we are not all to go under.

Following the work of earlier writers, Segundo offers a simple pastoral approach to "evangelizing" that applies to the problems we have discussed here. He would employ a basic kerygmatic method which: first, communicates only the essentials of the Christian message; second, communicates them *as* "good news"; third, adds nothing except at a pace that will allow the essential element to remain precisely that.[14] For example, all evangelists, says Segundo, must begin with *listening*, if the process is not to end up in more prefabricated formulas. Hence, even so basic a kerygma as "God raised his son, Jesus Christ, from the dead," may be alien to many cultural contexts. Perhaps a more fundamental statement, "No love is lost on this earth," may have to be a starting point for cross-cultural communi-

---

[13]Segundo, *Hidden Motives*, p. 26.
[14]Ibid., pp. 11–120.

cation of the Gospel.[15] Some years ago, I tried to propose a simplified approach to evangelization, using only the basic teachings about the person of Jesus, His oneness with the Father, redemption as liberation, and agapaic love.[16] Now, with better knowledge of problems in language and symbol as well as outlook, I would see even this much as only for later catechesis. Evangelization is thus more than a praxis of service and God-inspired reconciliation with much less effort to communicate conceptual content. In this light, I would agree with Vincent Donovan that "pre-evangelization," or *preparing* people to hear the Gospel, is of little use among peoples either of different worldview or of a condition dominated by oppression.[17] Every person of reasonably sound mind is ready to hear the basic message of the Good News that God loves them and wants them to love everyone else. The message will no doubt sting and gall at first, but so it does with all of us in the challenges it issues.

If the Church wishes to look toward new indigenous forms of Christianity, then it will have to, late as it is, adopt much the kind of listening posture of a Neihardt and become gradually a part of the Indian culture, through *Indians* gradually becoming the *Church*. As a missionary Church we have to realize even more deeply how little we understand traditional Native American culture and worldview, and about the damage it has sustained. In fact, neither side, as a rule, understands the other, although Indians have a much longer history of learning how to *react* to us, than we have of learning to react to them. Perhaps Neihardt grasped at least this much about the religious picture — that deep communication between Christian missions and tribal people was rare. This may have had something to do with his omission of the Christian element from his writings on Black Elk.

I do not intend here to abdicate the role of missionary of the Good News, since I believe in the unique offer of love there is in Jesus Christ. Nor would I deny that the Gosepl must finally challenge and even confront every culture. What a missionary must beware of, however, is allowing any merely human or cultural reality to make preemptory

[15]Ibid., p. 114.

[16]Carl Starkloff, *The People of the Center* (New York: Seabury Press, 1974), pp. 130–139.

[17]Donovan, *Christianity Rediscovered*, p. 55.

demands in the name of Christianity. If Christ is truly for all peoples, then His salvation can be expressed in many ways. For example, because they have a more horizontal and social sense of both wrongdoing and forgiveness than does the traditional European Christianity, Native Americans may have to work with this kind of understanding of Jesus Christ, and through this understanding come to the Father as God of all peoples. In this kind of reflection, we have the seeds of a richer soteriology. Moreover, while missionaries embrace Christ as the Son of God and unique in their lives, it may often be necessary to their ministry to accept that such a belief develops slowly, and that people can indeed be saved, and even be part of the Church, long before there is such a developed Christology.

Christianity does offer liberation, salvation, and healing to Native American people, but this can happen only if that healing process takes place through a church which they can recognize as their own and live in as within a new kind of sacred hoop. As Indian missions move toward becoming real *churches* (and most Catholic missions for reasons beyond the scope of this article are not even within sight of this goal), the "sending churches" will recede, like John the Baptist, into the background. While the process of becoming a church goes on, the mission bodies will strive to create a deepening sense of selfhood and independence in mission peoples. They will, for example, waste no time in developing a sense and practice of "mutuality," to use a word so well-explained by David Bosch.[18] Mutuality describes what should be the growing relationship between sending churches and local mission bodies, or "infant" churches. All parties involved learn in this way what resources each group or person has to offer, not only to the mission church group but also to the Church as a whole. These resources must be welcomed and allowed to develop. In turn, mission peoples have to learn that they are not to be passive recipients, as many have sadly learned to be, of an alien gospel and culture.

In such a body as the rejuvenated Catholic Tekakwitha Conference, for example, some 400 native peoples of the United States and Canada, along with over two hundred persons who now serve them,

[18]See David J. Bosch, "Towards True Mutuality: Exchanging the Same Commodities or Supplementing Each Other's Needs?" *Missionology*, VI (July 1978), pp. 283–296.

have made themselves heard by the hierarchy and the Church at large. Workshops within this conference are hammering out authentic Indian approaches to areas such as catechesis, family life and development, liturgy, social justice, and just plain having fun. These Christian Indians are finding true "power," not only as the grace of God, but concretized as a voice within the Church and through the Church to the world. They are gradually learning for themselves and showing to others that the vision of Black Elk — the Sacred Tree and the Hoop of the Nation, both in a much deeper and wider sense — need not die.

The new synthesis of Indian life, presuming there is to be one within Christianity, will be achieved by overcoming the devastating experiences of alienation from the culture which brought the Church with it, as well as finding final release from the alienation of the native culture itself. Such a synthesis can be helped by some of the insights of liberation theology as applied within the American context. Liberation and praxis strive to bring the message of Christ down from the stratospheric heights to which theology and dogma have often consigned it, into the lives and struggles of the people. But even this brand of theology must overcome the grave danger of simply becoming another foreign import. If there is to be a true Amerindian Church which will contribute something towards eliminating the divisions in both tribal life and in Christianity, it cannot be one of weeping old men with only memories to live on, beautiful as these are. It must be a vigorous community bearing a message of challenge for the world, grounded within a solid cultural life. It will have its own native ministry, its own theology, its own laws, its own worship forms. It will show the world the spiritual values that have lived within its own history over the millenia, and proclaim that Christ has come to fulfill these values.

Such a Christian Indian community will issue a challenge to people of whatever religious persuasion to overcome their differences and build an overarching worldview that all might live by, incorporating the insights of many branches of knowledge and human traditions. It may well be that the ancient philosophies and mythologies of traditional native tribes can tell us more about this kind of unification than either we or they have yet imagined. For the American Indian worldview, tribal or not, has always been possessed by the desire for integration, unification, and balance. Now Christianity has the opportunity to learn from this tradition and thus make good its claims of universality.

John Neihardt, in entering into the world of the Sioux medicine man, demonstrated that it was possible for people of different cultures to enter into a synthesis of meaning and understanding. His faithful reproduction of the substance of Sioux religion, visions, and symbolism has given us a great body of knowledge which will be increasingly useful in formulating the eventual religious synthesis that Indians promise. If we remain as faithful to our tasks as he was to his, there should be no question that we can produce sometime in the future an understanding of the reality of the one great hoop that encloses all God's children.

Index

The following is a name index. For subject entries see under Black Elk, Nicolaus, or Neihardt, John G.